Lose Weight Fast!

Lose Weight Fast!

Susie Burrell

BANTAM

SYDNEY AUCKLAND TORONTO NEW YORK LONDON

A Bantam book
Published by Random House Australia Pty Ltd
Level 3, 100 Pacific Highway, North Sydney NSW 2060
www.randomhouse.com.au

First published by Bantam in 2012

Addresses for companies within the Random House Group can be found at
www.randomhouse.com.au/offices

National Library of Australia
Cataloguing-in-Publication Entry

Burrell, Susie.
Lose weight fast/Susie Burrell.

ISBN 978 1 74275 519 9 (pbk.)

Weight loss.
Body weight – Regulation.
Reducing diets – Recipes.

613.25

Internal design and typesetting by Midland Typesetters, Australia
Printed in Australia by Griffin Press, an accredited ISO AS/NZS 14001:2004
Environmental Management System printer

The paper this book is printed on is certified against the Forest Stewardship Council® Standards. Griffin Press holds FSC chain of custody certification SGS-COC-005088. FSC promotes environmentally responsible, socially beneficial and economically viable management of the world's forests.

To all of my wonderful clients, who for the past 10 years have let me into your lives, trusted me and taught me everything I know

CONTENTS

The sooner you take responsibility for your food, your lifestyle choices and your body, the sooner you will get your weight under control, for life.

When slow and steady just doesn't cut it

❀ *Who wouldn't want to lose weight fast?*

Given the choice, wouldn't you want to lose weight fast? Sure, you may have spent months if not years eating too much and not exercising enough, which is why you have gained weight in the first place, but once you decide that you want the extra weight gone, you want it gone as quickly as possible. In a society that expects quick-fix solutions and instant gratification, it is no surprise to learn that when people decide to embark on a weight loss program, they want to lose weight fast. Unfortunately, as much as we may desire this outcome, it is not so easy, as many of us know all too well.

So, can you really lose weight fast if you want to and need to?

The answer is that you can, *if* you do it the right way. First and foremost you will need to accept that there are certain variables such as metabolism and genetics that need to be considered. Second, you need to be realistic. You physically cannot lose 20 kilos in a week, but you may be able to lose 2 or even 5 kilos in that time frame, depending on how committed you are and how your body responds to certain diet and exercise regimes.

Lose Weight Fast is for people who want or need to shed kilos quickly but who want to do it the right way – in a way that is safe and that ultimately produces sustainable results.

This book shows you what you can realistically achieve when it comes to losing weight over 3–5 days, a couple of weeks, a month, or 3 to 6 months. You will find here all the tips and tricks of the nutrition trade that will enable you to lose weight as quickly as possible without doing any long-term damage to your metabolic rate – and without leaving you more obsessed with diets and weight loss than you may have been before. So whether you have a few days, a couple of weeks or even 6 months to shed your unwanted kilos, or whether you are dealing with a dreaded weight rebound after previously losing weight, you will find all the tools you need right here. You will learn exactly how to lose weight by making the appropriate diet and exercise choices day-to-day, and ultimately you will be able to take control of your food and your weight once and for all.

Some important things to know

✿ *There are some things we can change, and some things we cannot.*

Losing weight fast or losing weight in general and then keeping it off is a complex process, and often the behaviours that we think will result in weight loss are not the ones that will actually get results. There are two physiological principles that we need to constantly remember as we seek to burn body fat as efficiently as possible: 'optimising metabolism' and 'training efficiently'.

Optimising metabolism

Metabolism is a term that is frequently used in articles and books about weight loss but rarely do such reports talk about the role metabolism plays in our ability to stay in control of our weight as we get older. As we age, our body naturally becomes less efficient at burning calories, which means that our metabolic rate, the number of calories our cells burn each day, slows down. This is why we gain weight gradually even when we exercise regularly and consume a similar number of calories each day.

When we are actively trying to lose weight, it is a commonly held belief that we need to eat fewer calories, and indeed this is the case, but what is also crucial to know is that if we cut back on calories by too great an extent metabolic rate will also slow, as the cells' engines slow down to conserve energy and weight loss may come to a halt. You may have even experienced this firsthand if you have ever significantly reduced your calorie intake to less than 1000 calories a day and found that you didn't lose weight any faster or didn't lose any weight at all. While we can reduce calories safely, as shown throughout *Lose Weight Fast*, if you keep in the forefront of your mind the concept that 'you need fuel to burn body fat', and remember that your calorie intake must not go below a certain level (which varies from person to person), no matter what, to protect metabolic rate from slowing, you will have a much better chance of losing weight successfully.

Training efficiently

While calorie intake is important for weight loss, the most powerful thing we can do to increase the cells' ability to burn body fat in the long term and optimise our metabolic rate is to 'train' our cells to burn more efficiently via the right kind of exercise.

To give our cells the boost they need to start burning calories more efficiently and to keep doing this, we need to challenge them regularly. The way we achieve this is by training at an intense level that increases our heart rate significantly (a walk in the park just won't cut it). For this reason, throughout *Lose Weight Fast* you will see that the word 'training' is used rather than 'exercise'. Unlike exercise, training refers specifically to participating in activity that significantly raises your heart rate and gives you the metabolic boost you need for the cells to start burning fat more effectively. In this book training is also differentiated from walking and moving, 'moving' being the term used to describe incidental activity (the physical activity we perform as part of our daily life, such as walking to the bus stop or taking the stairs instead of the lift). Throughout *Lose*

Weight Fast you will discover how you can work towards achieving the right balance between moving and training in your life so that you will be able to lose weight and, most importantly, know what you need to do to keep it off for good.

Preparing to lose weight

✿ *Preparation and planning are the keys to successful weight loss.*

How much do you want to lose, how quickly do you want to lose it and how strict are you prepared to be?

These are key questions. A great deal of research has gone into the physiology of weight loss. We don't know everything, but the fundamental processes are well understood. To give yourself the best chance of success, the first and most important thing you need to do is to **be very clear about how much weight you want to lose and in what time frame**. Only then can you choose the program that is most likely to work for you. Clearly, a program tailored for a 60 kilogram female who wants to shed 3 kilos will not be the same as one designed for a 120 kilogram female who needs to lose 40 kilos.

When you have 3–5 days

You probably don't need to be told that you are not going to achieve a great deal in such a short period. This is insufficient time for the body to burn a significant amount of fat, which means that any weight you lose is going to be water and the result of your muscles being depleted of carbohydrate. For many people, though, the feeling of lightness that comes from eating an extremely light, largely fluid-based diet for a brief period of time is sufficient reward and can act as a kick-start for a longer-term weight loss program.

When you have 1–2 weeks

Over a 1–2 week period it is possible to lose a couple of kilos of weight by strictly limiting your carbohydrate and calorie intake. While some of the weight you lose will be fluid, as naturally occurs when you cut back on carbohydrates, some will also be fat as you move past the initial 2–3 days of the program. The most important thing to remember when deciding to follow a strict dietary program is that such programs are generally insufficient in calories and carbs to provide the body with the essential nutrients it needs to function optimally. For this reason they should only be followed for a short period – ideally no longer than 1–2 weeks at a time. In order to achieve these weight loss results, you are also going to have to be strict – there will be no room for treats, extras or alcohol during a 1 or 2 week weight loss program.

When you have a month

Once you shift your weight loss focus from a week or two to a month, much more can be achieved. A 4 week period is a sufficient period of time to lose several kilos, bearing in mind that a tightly controlled calorie intake coupled with regular exercise can see weight losses of between half a kilo and a kilo a week. Unlike the more intense regimes used for several days or a couple of weeks, which strictly limit carbohydrates, a 4 week program needs to include more calories and more carbohydrates to ensure that the body has the minimum amount of both necessary to prevent the starvation response. The starvation response occurs when calories and/or carbohydrates are kept very low for longer than a few days at a time and the body responds by burning fewer calories to conserve energy. As a result, weight loss slows.

When you have 3 months

This is a great period of time to dedicate to weight loss, as you can achieve significant results and lose as much as 10 kilos when you have this much time to work with. As the period of time you commit to weight loss increases, so too do your program options. For example, you may begin using a stricter approach that sees you lose a couple of kilos quickly, and then move on to a higher calorie plan that allows you to lose more moderate amounts of weight, or you may choose a more gradual program that results in slow steady weight loss over the 3 month period.

There are two main factors that need to be considered when you have longer to commit to weight loss. The first is that there may be times when you lose momentum and go 'off track', and the second is that you may experience a weight loss 'plateau', which may require adjustments to both your diet and training programs at certain time points. Learning to manage these scenarios throughout your weight loss program is the key to continuing to lose weight over a 3 month period and moving towards your goal weight.

When you have 6 months

When you are looking at shifting a significant amount of weight, such as 20 or 30 kilos, or if you have been battling weight issues for many years, you need to give yourself a realistic amount of time to achieve your goal. When individuals are seen to lose large amounts of weight relatively quickly, as happens in 'reality' television shows, it is important to remember that these people are usually living a life in which their sole focus is weight loss. They are able to dedicate themselves to following a very controlled diet and training for many hours each day, all under expert supervision, which few of us in the real world are able (or want) to do. For this reason, you need to give yourself at least 4–6 months to shift 20–30 kilos. This amount of time will ensure that you develop sound food and training patterns over time that you can easily maintain once you have lost your excess weight. It also gives you plenty of time to closely examine the various patterns of behaviour that may have been contributing to your extra weight directly or indirectly, so that, ideally, you can learn to manage them in the long term.

Getting into the right headspace for weight loss

❖ *Are you mentally ready to commit to weight loss –* really *ready?*

The headspace you are in when you first begin a new weight loss program is crucially important – even more important than your knowledge of nutrition and fat metabolism. So, before you begin your weight loss journey, it is very useful to reflect and undertake some self-evaluation to make sure that you are in the right headspace to fully commit to a new program.

Taking responsibility for yourself

There can be a lot of blame in life. We blame our parents for not teaching us the right eating habits, or our workplace for making us fat. Or we blame our partner for not helping us at home so that we have sufficient time to exercise as regularly as we need to, or our best friend for tempting us with high-fat treats during a coffee date and deliberately throwing us off track with our program.

To take control of both our food and exercise programs we need to accept that there will always be factors that from time to time impact on our ability to remain focused and on task, and then redirect our emotional energy into finding specific, practical ways around whatever is hindering our weight loss efforts.

Any dietitian will tell you that the clients who always attend their appointments, who are open to new ideas and focus simply on how they are going to make a new diet or exercise change work are the ones who do well. Clients who spend their appointment time explaining all the reasons why they can't do something, or giving excuses for not having done the things they needed to do to lose weight, don't.

Taking responsibility for yourself also means accepting that there are certain things about eating well and exercising regularly that may not seem particularly 'easy' or 'fun' but that you must take on board if you truly want to be leaner, fitter and healthier. It means accepting that you are going to have to make some changes and ultimately some sacrifices as well.

The sooner you are able to shift your focus from resentment about what you have to do to a positive mindset where you look for ways in which you can do what you need to do to get your weight and life under control, you will start to make progress.

Developing a framework

Weight loss programs usually work because they give people a framework that helps them to get organised, to structure their eating habits and to develop a schedule for training regularly. When they fail, as they sometimes do, it is usually because the framework is not suited to the individual in the long term.

The trick is to develop a framework that suits you and your family. This may mean that you eat early during the week, or only drink alcohol on weekends. It may mean that you see a personal trainer 5 days a week or it may mean that you walk twice a day for the rest of your life. There are no rules, but unless you work towards establishing your own framework for weight control you are likely to try program after program with no long-term results.

Focusing on metabolism

It is relatively easy to lose weight – if you consistently cut down on your calories and become more active you should lose at least small amounts of weight over a long-term period. But if you really want to rid yourself of weight issues, you need to focus on increasing your metabolic rate as well. Whether we like it or not, our metabolic rate declines as we get older, which means that we ultimately burn fewer calories if we do the same things we have always done. This in turn means that ultimately we will have to eat less if we are to maintain the same weight.

The good news is that focusing on increasing metabolic rate, and preventing this scenario, as part of your weight loss program is actually very easy to do – it is about eating and training the right way. It is also about learning to identify the body's natural hunger and fullness signals and about becoming leaner and fitter with intense but targeted training.

Programming yourself to eat less

In a world that is constantly encouraging us to eat more, we need to focus on constantly eating less – the conflict is all too clear. The scary thing is that people can be eating almost double the number of calories that they need at some mealtimes and as a result are petrified that cutting back will leave them hungry.

Instead of eating according to our natural hunger and satiety (fullness) signals, many of us eat the way we have been programmed to eat for a range of reasons other than hunger over many years – by parents, friends, what we see in the movies or on television, advertisements – and sometimes we eat just because the food is there. For example, we may always have two slices of toast for breakfast, even if we are not especially hungry, or we may always eat a whole sandwich at lunchtime, regardless of whether it is large or small. Much the same can be said for dessert – we may only want a taste, but we eat the whole thing for fear of wasting it or because this is what we 'always' do.

To successfully control our weight in an environment in which food is readily available and often served up in large portions, we need to reprogram ourselves. The first thing we need to do is to get into the habit of considering how much food we really need on any particular occasion and then control our portions accordingly. It takes time to achieve this, but once it becomes a habit most people are surprised to discover how little food they really need, and how much extra they have been eating.

Focusing on wellbeing

Many clients who seek dietary counselling are unhappy not only with their weight but also with their life. Out of control food and exercise habits are often a marker for disorganised, overwhelming lives.

The good news is that it is not uncommon for a complete shift to occur once a client takes control of their food and their body. They then start to focus on making necessary changes in other areas of their life, whether it is their relationships, their work, their home life or their financial situation.

Once we have achieved a balance in relation to the way we eat and the time we commit to looking after our body, we also tend to be healthier, happier and more energised – and therefore in a better space physically and psychologically to develop full and fulfilling lives. So, as you progress through this journey, remember that at some level it is not just about weight loss, **it is about you and the person you are waiting to become once you are free of weight worries.**

What are the keys to successful weight loss?

❀ *To optimise weight loss, you need to keep an eye on both your calories and your carbs.*

Every year, billions of dollars are spent on weight loss programs that promise the seemingly elusive goal of rapid yet sustainable weight loss. At least 95 per cent of these diets and programs fail. They fail for a number of reasons, one of the main ones being that they are not sustainable in the long term – you start them and lose a kilo or two, and then real life gets in the way and you are back where you started. They also fail because they include foods that you would not usually eat and because you are often left hungry and unsatisfied. Perhaps most important of all, they fail because, though you may not be aware of it, you set yourself up to fail. All too often we assume that any program we adopt will only need to be followed for a few days or weeks at the most, and we then return to our less than ideal food and exercise habits and regain most if not all of the weight we worked very hard to lose.

While you can lose weight relatively quickly if you need or want to, there is a right and a wrong way to do it. The wrong way will see your energy, nutrition and ultimately your metabolism compromised. While you may lose weight in the short term, the chances of your keeping it off in the long term are slim. On the other hand, if you adopt a program that has been developed to allow you to drop the maximum number of kilos with minimal damage to your body's energy systems, you will be in a much better position to reap the benefits in the long term.

The first thing you need to understand is that there are a minimal number of calories your body requires to function. If your calorie intake falls below this level, your body's energy systems will not be able to burn calories as efficiently as they otherwise could, metabolism will slow and this will hinder your weight loss efforts. While the number of calories will differ depending on gender, body size and activity levels, for a small female it is likely to be between 1200 and 1500 calories, and for a male between 1600 and 1800 calories. This means that any calorie prescription you are planning to use for longer than a week or two needs to include at least this basic number of calories.

The other key to dieting is to understand that at times you will need to adjust your carbohydrate intake. Carbohydrates are the primary fuel for muscle, and many weight loss programs get their seemingly rapid results by drastically cutting back on carbs (in the form of bread, cereals, fruit and sugars), which causes the body to release the fluid that the carbohydrate normally holds in the muscles. This will result in almost instant weight loss of 1–2 kilos (but remember that it is fluid, not fat). If, however, an extremely low-carb diet is followed for an extended period of time, this inhibits the body's primary fat-burning system, which is counterproductive.

As a rule of thumb, an adult will need a total of at least 80–100 grams of carbohydrate a day to prevent issues with the functioning of these energy systems in the long term, although it is safe to manipulate carbohydrate intake for limited periods during a weight loss program in order to enhance fat burning and weight loss. The key is to know the right way of doing this.

The one exception to this rule is when people are put on what are known as 'very low-calorie diets'. These diets are scientifically formulated programs in which all meals are replaced by formulated shakes and products that contain all the nutrients that regular meals contain but have minimal calories. Keeping calories and in particular carbohydrates at specific low levels shifts the body's metabolism into burning fat for energy instead of glucose, thus optimising fat loss. While this may sound like an appealing option, these diets are extreme and can be difficult to follow, and as such are usually reserved for extreme cases where a person needs to lose weight rapidly, such as pre-surgery, and nothing else has worked.

Now that you have a basic understanding of the underlying principles, you will notice that the first two programs in *Lose Weight Fast* manipulate both calories and carbs to get more rapid results (in 3–5 days and 1–2 weeks respectively), whereas the one-month, 3 month and 6 month programs are less aggressive and aim rather for slow, sustainable weight loss. While you can interchange these programs, always remember the importance of not putting your metabolic rate under too much pressure in the long term. This means that you should limit the more extreme regimes to a week or two at a time, and follow them no more than a couple of times per year.

When you have 3–5 days

❖ *'This dress would look so much better if my stomach was a little flatter.'*

You would be surprised how many people leave it until the very last minute to lose weight before an important event, occasion or even season. When you consider that we see so many advertisements for commercial weight loss programs making claims of clients losing amounts of 5 or even 10 kilos in as little as a week, it's only natural that we think it must be possible to shed weight this quickly.

Elite-level athletes who are required to weigh in prior to competition, such as lightweight rowers and boxers, are able to shed as much as 2–5 kilos in 3–5 days using various techniques that deplete the body of both fluid and carbohydrate, although they usually do this under expert supervision. **You too can use these techniques,** as long as you remember that while the scales may show a distinct drop, the weight you are shedding within such a short period is usually not fat but fluid, and that you will quickly regain the fluid and the weight once you return to your regular habits. It is strictly a short-term measure with short-term results.

Of course, most people who are anxious to shed weight quickly, such as for a special occasion, are not fussed about whether they are losing fat or fluid as long as they see results. So what can you realistically achieve in 3–5 days?

The body of an average-sized female weighing between 55 and 70 kilos is composed of somewhere between 35 and 40 kilos of muscle mass, depending on her age, whether or not she trains regularly, her hormones and her genetics. One of the primary roles of muscle mass is to store carbohydrate in the form of glycogen, which is used to fuel the muscle. As glycogen also stores a significant amount of water, the greater the volume of muscle mass you have, and the more carbohydrate you have stored, the heavier you will be. In the average person, stored fuel and the fluid that accompanies it can account for as much as 2–3 kilos of body weight.

A low-carbohydrate eating plan such as that shown below contains less than 50 grams of total carbohydrate, whereas a standard eating plan would often contain as much as 150–200 grams of carbohydrate. Over a 3–5 day period of following such a low-carb diet, the stored carbohydrate (in the form of glycogen) that you have been holding in your muscles will be broken down to be used as energy to fuel the muscle. As the fluid that has been stored with this glycogen is released, this results in a rapid (though temporary) weight loss of up to 2–3 kilos, although this will differ between individuals, depending on their body weight and how much extra muscle mass they are carrying.

Sample low-carb eating plan

	FOOD	TOTAL CARBS (g)
Breakfast	Protein shake	2
Mid-morning	1 cup of berries and 1 slice of cheese	5
Lunch	Tuna salad	5
Mid-afternoon	Handful of nuts	0
Dinner	Grilled chicken and vegetables	10
	Total carbs	22

People who take this approach further and follow a low-carb diet exclusively for 3–4 weeks can see rapid weight loss of up to 5 kilos. Although this kind of diet is likely to leave you dehydrated and low in energy, for some people the weight loss and the fact that they feel less bloated and puffy are enough to motivate them to keep going with such an extreme regime.

It is fine to go low-carb for a short (3–5 days) period of time. As long as you are consuming plenty of low-calorie vegetables and salad, as well as some lean protein such as fish or eggs at each meal in order to get your essential nutrients such as iron, zinc and vitamin B_{12}, you will be getting a reasonably good intake of nutrients even though your carb intake is low. Low-carb diets can be particularly valuable for people who have dieted off and on for a long period of time and who may as a result have various metabolic issues, including insulin resistance, which can make weight loss challenging. (Insulin resistance is discussed on page 201.) In these more extreme cases, a low-carb diet can act as a 'kick-start' when a traditional calorie-reduced, low-fat diet does not appear to be working.

Low-carb diets are usually also low in calories, simply because they restrict or eliminate so many foods, including fruit, bread, rice, cereal, pasta, sugars and grains. When followed for more than a week or two, however, low-calorie diets are known to reduce the metabolic rate, which means that over time the body becomes less efficient at burning calories. This is why you should resort to such an extreme regime only occasionally and for a short period of time, such as a week-long weight loss kick-start or for times when you need a flat tummy ASAP.

The good thing about wanting to lose weight in the very short term is that it usually means you will be highly motivated. You want to look good in a special outfit or for a big occasion, and that is usually enough to keep you on track with even the strictest diet or exercise plan.

When you are planning to embark on an intense weight loss phase, always keep in mind that such strategies are not good for your health in the long term. **Constantly limiting calories and carbohydrates places the body under significant stress,** even though you may not be aware of it. For this reason, once you do drop those few pesky kilos, aim to keep them off rather than going straight back to your old habits. It is always much easier to prevent weight gain than to get weight off once the extra kilos are there.

Getting started

1. ELIMINATE THE CARBS

Bread, rice, cereal and pasta as well as fruits, juices and sugars are all plant-based foods that consist primarily of carbohydrates. As carbohydrates attract fluid within the muscle, **eliminating carbohydrates from the diet for a few days will** give weight loss a little kick-start and allow you to **see a drop of a kilo or two on the scales.** This means eating only low-calorie vegetables and fruit and a small amount of lean protein, as shown in the low-carb diet here.

TYPICAL MODERATE-CARB DIET	CARBS (g)	LOW-CARB DIET	CARBS (g)
Breakfast: Cereal and milk	45	Strip (1 egg) omelette	4
Mid-morning: Fruit and yoghurt	50	Cheese and rye crackers	6
Lunch: Tuna sandwich	30	Strip tuna salad	5
Mid-afternoon: Trail mix	30	Berries and nuts	10
Dinner: Spaghetti bolognaise	60	Grilled steak and salad	5
Total	215	Total	30

STRIP OMELETTE

1 medium egg

¼ cup low-fat milk

Canola oil spray

4 cherry tomatoes

2 small mushrooms

½ cup English spinach

20 g reduced-fat fetta cheese

1 Beat egg with milk; pour into a warm pan sprayed with oil.

2 Cook until base of egg is set, then add vegetables down the middle and fold half of the omelette over the filling.

3 Sprinkle with fetta and serve.

Serves 1

STRIP TUNA SALAD

100 g tuna in oil, drained, or red salmon

2 cups rocket or English spinach leaves

6 cherry tomatoes

1 Lebanese cucumber, sliced

½ cup roasted pumpkin

½ red capsicum, sliced

Fat-free dressing

Mix all ingredients together for a delicious salad.

Serves 1

2. LOAD UP ON VEGETABLES

If we all simply ate a lot more low-calorie vegetables and salad, far fewer of us would have weight issues. Leaving that aside, utilising the low-calorie, high-water content of vegetables and salads during a period of rapid weight loss is crucial not only to keep your calorie and carb intake low, but also to help you feel full and satisfied even though you are not eating a lot. Generally speaking, **the majority of vegetables and salad have almost negligible calories, so yes, you can pretty much eat as much of them as you like.** The few exceptions are sweet potato, potato and sweet corn, which have a much higher carbohydrate and calorie content.

Carb/calorie content of low-calorie vegetables

SALAD VEGETABLES (PER CUP, RAW)	CARBS (g)	CALORIES
Broccoli	<1	20
Pumpkin	10	70
Carrot	7	45
Tomato	4	30
Red capsicum	4	30
Cucumber	3	16
Peas	10	100
Green beans	3	30
Beetroot	10	60
Celery	1	15

When your goal is to drop kilos over just a few days, aim to consume at least 4–5 cups of vegetables (excluding sweet potato, potato and sweet corn), salad or soup each day. It is an easy thing to focus on, and it will also help you to rid your body of any extra fluid you may have been retaining from eating salt-heavy processed and fast foods. Include vegetables such as tomatoes and mushrooms in your breakfast to bulk up your meal with minimal extra calories. Snack on vegetables such as celery and cucumber, and base both your main meals around salad and vegetables, whether in the form of soups, salad or cooked or fresh vegetables.

STRIP SOUP

1 small onion, finely chopped

2 cloves garlic, finely chopped

Olive oil

2 leeks, white end only, finely chopped

3 zucchinis, sliced

4–5 cups water

2 cups salt-reduced chicken or vegetable stock

1 cup low-fat milk

1 Sauté onion and garlic in a small amount of olive oil. Add leek and zucchini and cook until soft.

2 Add water and stock; mix to blend, bring to the boil, then turn heat down and add milk. Once heated through, transfer to a food processor and blend and serve.

Serves 1

3. EAT CLEAN

Eating clean simply means eating your food in as natural a state as possible. This means eating meats, salads and vegetables plain, without extra sauces, butter and salt. It means adding other whole foods, such as avocado, fruits, and herbs and spices, to flavour foods. It means opting for clear fluids such as water and herbal tea instead of our usual choices of sweetened drinks, including milk-based coffee and tea, soy drinks, smoothies and juices. Cleansing the palate of intense flavour and sweetness plays a subtle but extremely powerful role in changing eating behaviour in the long term. Once you have eliminated intense flavours from your diet, you will find that plain foods, including vegetables, dairy foods and even fruit, start to taste sweeter and richer. **Natural, whole foods are more filling, and once you get used to them you will find you no longer crave salty, fatty, sugary foods.** In the long term this means it becomes much easier to eat the kinds of foods that will help you control your weight.

An example of regular eating versus clean eating

REGULAR EATING	CLEAN EATING
Salad with oil-based dressing	Salad with vinegar and herbs
Soup seasoned with salt	Soup flavoured with herbs
Tea with milk	Herbal tea
Fruit juice	Water with lemon
Crackers with margarine	Crackers with avocado
Tea with milk and sugar	Green tea

4. ADD IN SOME LIGHT PROTEIN

A low-carb diet can be tricky, as our natural tendency is to replace the carbs with extra protein, such as a giant steak or a large piece of Atlantic salmon, or an omelette made with multiple eggs, or an entire pack of processed meat. While it is essential to have some protein on a low-carb diet, large servings, particularly of the heavier proteins such as red meat, will simply increase the fat content of your diet. This will slow digestion and can leave you feeling heavier and even constipated.

For this reason, while you should include protein in a 3–5 day program, you should eat small portions of lighter protein foods that are digested relatively quickly. Include 50–100 gram serves of the following light protein-based choices in each meal of your program, and consider that, as we usually eat far more than we think, you may need to weigh your protein serves to keep your calories low.

PROTEIN FOOD	SERVING SIZE PER MEAL
Egg	1 small egg
Chicken breast	50–70 g
White fish	100 g
Red fish	50–70 g
Tofu	50 g
Prawns	5–7 medium
Tuna/salmon	Small can
Lentils, chickpeas	½ cup cooked

5. USE A MEAL REPLACEMENT SHAKE

One of the main issues when you are following a low-carb diet is keeping your blood glucose levels regulated so that you don't 'go low' and crave sugars, which potentially leave you vulnerable to hunger and binge eating. **One useful strategy to adopt during a period of quick weight loss is to replace a meal with a shake**. A shake can either be a protein-based shake or a 'liquid meal', a controlled-calorie meal replacement that contains about 200 calories, a serve of protein (12–20 grams) as well as having a full micronutrient profile. Such protein-rich formulations will help to keep you full, but as they are usually liquid shakes they are also digested quickly, helping to keep the bulk of food in your stomach minimal. Some programs suggest replacing more than one meal each day with a shake, but you should get good results from replacing just one.

One option is to replace breakfast with a shake, or alternatively your evening meal. The evening option may be a good choice if you find that you often struggle to stay on track with your dinner choices, or if you find yourself constantly snacking after dinner. The higher protein content of the shake should fill you up and help regulate your appetite.

6. USE FIBRE THE RIGHT WAY

While loading up on fibre-rich foods to clear out your digestive tract is a good idea overall, you need to be aware that some types of fibre produce gas as they are being digested, which can leave you feeling bloated and gassy rather than slim and light. For this reason, any heavy, fibrous vegetable is best avoided during a rapid weight loss program. This will mean shifting your focus from fibre-rich foods to low-bulk foods to remove as much residue from the gut as possible.

Foods that can cause bloating

Broccoli

Cauliflower

Broad beans

Chickpeas

Kidney beans

Onions

Garlic

Mushrooms

7. SWITCH TO LIGHT FOODS

For the final day or two of your strip weight loss plan, switching to liquids and low-bulk foods is a sure-fire way to rid your digestive tract of as much bulk and weight as possible. This does not mean that you have to resort to honey in water or any weird juice diet; it simply means using liquid meal drinks, soups and other light foods that will allow you to feel full with minimal bulk in your tummy.

Sample low-bulk eating plan

Breakfast: Meal replacement drink or protein shake

Mid-morning: Herbal tea and a punnet of berries

Lunch: Large bowl of vegetable soup

Mid-afternoon: Small vegetable juice with 2 rice crackers and 2 teaspoons of no added sugar peanut butter

Dinner: Large bowl of homemade vegetable soup with 2 rice thins and a 95 g can of tuna

8. ADD IN SOME BRAN

One of the issues with any low-calorie meal plan, particularly one that eliminates much of the grain bulk from the diet, is constipation. **Being constipated means that you can be 1–2 kilos heavier than you otherwise would be simply because there is a build-up in your digestive tract,** which can also leave you feeling uncomfortable. To avoid this, the one thing you can do as part of your quick weight loss program is to include a small handful (⅓ cup) of wheat bran every day. It doesn't matter whether you blend it into a shake or munch on it as a snack with plenty of water; it is simply an aid to ensure that you continue to go to the bathroom regularly even on a restricted eating plan.

9. TAKE A PROBIOTIC

There is a growing amount of evidence to show that gut health is extremely important when it comes to immune function. As any low-calorie eating plan will put pressure on both your immune system and your digestive tract, it is a wise move to take a probiotic daily when you are severely restricting your food intake. This can be a capsule supplement or yoghurt with live cultures.

10. INCLUDE SOME LIGHT EXERCISE

When you are on an extremely low-carb, low-calorie diet for a short period of time, it is important to limit yourself to light exercise only. Remember that you are basically starving your muscle of carbohydrate, so this is not the time to be pushing your muscle to work exceptionally hard. Stick to moderate-intensity activity such as walking or swimming. So, rather than flog yourself at the gym for an hour, break your exercise down into two 20-minute or 30-minute sessions of walking, swimming or gentle cycling. This will help to burn calories without putting excessive pressure on your body when it is already being significantly deprived of calories.

Your 3–5 day Super Strip Plan

DAY 1	DAY 2	DAY 3	DAY 4	DAY 5
Liquid meal replacement/ protein shake	Strip Omelette (p. 22) or similar 1 egg omelette	½ cup wheat bran + 1 cup skim milk	Liquid meal replacement/ protein shake	Liquid meal replacement/ protein shake
1 cup berries + ½ cup wheat bran	200 ml mixed vegetable juice	1 cup berries	100 g tub pears or peaches	1 cup fruit salad + ½ cup natural yoghurt
Large green salad with 50 g turkey breast + 1 tsp olive oil	Liquid meal replacement	Large salad + 95 g tuna in olive oil, drained, + ¼ avocado	2 rice cakes + ¼ avocado	Large salad + 50 g salmon + 2 rice cakes
2 rice cakes + 2 tsp no added sugar peanut butter	5 walnuts + 2 slices melon	Liquid meal replacement/ protein shake	⅓ cup wheat bran + 1 cup berries	Liquid meal replacement + ⅓ cup wheat bran
Bowl of Strip Soup (p. 24) + 100 g grilled white fish	Bowl of Strip Soup + 100 g grilled salmon	Bowl of Strip Soup	Bowl of Strip Soup	Bowl of Strip Soup

Now reap, and keep, the rewards

At the end of a 3–5 day period of low-carb, low-calorie eating based on a high intake of vegetables and salad you should have lost at least 2 kilos. You are likely to be feeling amazing and that the effort was all worth it. The most important thing to keep in mind at this point is that **going out and bingeing on high-carb, high-calorie food and lots of alcohol is the worst thing you can do.** Not only will your body cling on to every gram of carb that you eat for dear life, your poor stomach will not be used to such large volumes of food and you will very quickly feel sick. So, after 3–5 days grade up your food and carb intake slowly. Add a little extra food to your lunch and breakfast meals, but keep your evening meal small and based on lean protein and vegetables. This will ensure that you do not undo all your hard work and will put you on track for shedding those kilos not just in the short term but for good.

Sample follow-on diet

(Recommended for at least a week after your 3–5 day Strip Plan.)

Breakfast: Breakfast shake

Mid-morning: 1 piece of fruit + small skim milk coffee

Lunch: 2 corn or rye crackers with 95 g tuna and salad

Mid-afternoon: 10 nuts with 1 piece of fruit

Dinner: 100 g grilled protein with salad or vegetables

Tips and tricks for your Strip Plan

- The most important thing to remember is that this type of eating plan should be followed for no longer than 3–5 days.

- To ensure success, have all the foods you need on hand, make a large pot of Strip Soup, and have plenty of cut-up vegetables in the fridge to snack on.

- If you feel sick, tired or lethargic, remember that these symptoms should only last for a day or two at most.

- It is most important to allow yourself plenty of rest when you are following a very low-carb, low-calorie plan.

- Most of your meals should consist of low-calorie foods such as vegetables, salad and soups.

- If you find yourself feeling exceptionally hungry, have another bowl of low-calorie soup or an extra meal replacement.

- Avoid intense exercise and stick to short sessions of walking, swimming or gentle cycling.

- To prevent constipation, include some wheat bran in one of the meals in your eating plan every day.

- Drink plenty of green tea to help control any caffeine or sugar cravings.

- Try and avoid food-focused environments such as cafes, pubs and restaurants.

Strip checklist

1. Eliminate the carbs.
2. Load up on vegetables.
3. Eat clean.
4. Add in some light protein.
5. Use a meal replacement.
6. Use fibre the right way.
7. Switch to light foods.
8. Add in some bran.
9. Take a probiotic.
10. Include some light exercise.

When you have 1–2 weeks

❈ *'The school reunion is only 2 weeks away and I*
   really need to drop a couple of kilos before then.'

You may have a wedding or some other function to attend, you may want to look stunning in front of your ex-boyfriend, or you may simply know that you would feel so much better if you could just lose a kilo or two. Surely you can lose a couple of kilos in 2 weeks?

Now, losing a couple of kilos should not be difficult – you eat less, move more and bang, the weight is gone, but this is rarely the case. Often small treats slip in, we starve ourselves and then binge after a day or two and then we find ourselves back where we started. You can drop a couple of kilos over a week or two, but you must fully commit to the process. If you work hard and maintain some key dietary changes, you can do it – and we are talking here of shedding some body fat, not only or mainly fluid as in the 3–5 day program. Such a short time frame, though, does mean that you will have to focus and get serious. Just as an athlete needs to diet strictly prior to competition to achieve their performance goals, such is the focus required for this type of weight loss. **This means no alcohol, treats or extras for a week or two**. It also means sticking to a fairly rigid dietary routine.

Over the course of 1–2 weeks, you will be able to lose at least half a kilo to a kilo of body fat a week. While you will not need to completely eliminate carbs as suggested in the intense 3–5 day program, you will need to limit your carbs and combine this with some pretty intense training. If you do this, you will get great results. In fact, many people find that they drop a couple of kilos just by eliminating processed food from their diet and replacing it with plenty of fresh fruit and vegetables.

When committing to a relatively rigid dietary regime, you must be well organised. Make sure you have all the specific foods you need on hand so that you can stick with the program 100 per cent. This may mean staying in to eat and spending time on the weekends and in the evenings to prepare all your food in advance so that you are not tempted to grab quick options on the run. For busy people in particular, this step is crucial.

Getting in the right mindset to stay on track for 1–2 weeks

One of the obvious benefits of losing weight in a relatively short period of time is that it is far easier to stick with a plan for a week or two than for months and months. While it can be extremely motivating to drop a few kilos within a week or two, embarking on a strict regime is also a great opportunity to shift your mindset towards maintaining some of your new habits in the long term. So, yes, this is a diet that you can use to drop weight quickly for a particular occasion, but ultimately you can also use it as a baseline from which to build a lifestyle focused on moving your body more and paying a little more attention to what goes into your mouth on a daily basis.

Getting ready for the next 1–2 weeks

Buy all the foods you will need for the week ahead.

Cook a vegetable soup.

Wash and chop up your salad vegetables.

Clear out the cupboards and throw or give away any tempting foods or drinks.

Cook a spare meal in case you get home late one night.

Write up your weekly menu and place it on the fridge.

Weigh yourself and take your body measurements.

Schedule in your training sessions.

If you can, recruit a support person to join you on the program.

Cancel as many non-necessary social engagements as you can.

10 key strategies for your 1–2 week weight loss program

1. USE A MEAL REPLACEMENT

Meal replacements are scientifically formulated products that contain all the essential nutrients that a nutritionally balanced meal would contain but with far fewer calories. Originally, meal replacements were formulated by medical nutrition companies to induce rapid weight loss in severely obese people who needed to lose weight quickly in preparation for surgery. When people go on a diet consisting entirely of meal replacements, their intake of carbohydrate can be as low as 50 grams per day, which will result in the body going into a metabolic state called ketosis, in which it burns fat for energy instead of glucose (from carbohydrate). In other words, ketosis is a 'back-up' energy system that kicks in when the body is starved of its normal source of energy. While this approach will definitely work if you can follow it, it tends to be rather extreme.

The key feature of a meal replacement, whether it is a shake or a bar, is that it is low in calories (most have about 200 calories) but contains balanced quantities of carbohydrate and protein. The reason that meal replacements tend to give superior results compared to eating regular food is that it is very difficult to select regular food that offers the same nutrient profile with such a low level of calories. For example, a meal replacement would contain, on average, 20–25 grams of carbohydrates and 20 grams of protein with just 200 calories. This is the equivalent of a meal consisting of 2 slices of grain toast (24 grams of carbohydrate) and 2 poached eggs (20 grams of protein), which has almost double the number of calories.

Another benefit of using a meal replacement is that it eliminates the issue of extra calories slipping in – a larger slice of bread here, some extra butter there and before you know it you have significantly increased your calories and reduced the likelihood that you will be in a negative caloric balance and losing weight.

So, one of the most effective ways to use meal replacements is to use them to replace one or two of your meals. You may have seen many different types of shakes and diet products before, but a 'protein shake' is not the same thing; only a product that is referred to as a 'formulated meal replacement' will give you the metabolic benefits outlined here.

Practically, breakfast is the easiest and most popular meal to replace, as the high protein load (20 grams) appears to be of extra benefit during the morning when you are more likely to feel hungry. Another option some people find useful is to use one of these products to replace dinner, especially if you do not love cooking, find it difficult to eat early or have issues controlling your portion sizes at night. A third option is to use a meal replacement as a filling mid-afternoon snack. Although it contains more calories than the average mid-afternoon snack, for those who find their hunger and sugar cravings difficult to manage during the afternoon it's a much better option than bingeing on other foods, especially sweet foods. You need to be aware that you should use meal replacements at most twice a day, as their high protein content can contribute to constipation.

2. KEEP YOUR CALORIES AND CARBOHYDRATES LOW

'How low can you safely go?' That is the key question when it comes to cutting calories and rapid weight loss. Anyone who has dieted aggressively before will know that less is not necessarily better, particularly as you increase the amount of training and moving that you are doing. Think of your body as a machine, with the muscles representing the engine that burns fuel. If you take the petrol level too low, the car cannot run. That is pretty much the situation when we eat too few calories or carbohydrates. While you can drop the carbs for a short period of time to lower your carbohydrate stores and see a subsequent drop on the scales, if you are also dropping calories too low, below 1000–1200 calories, you will place too much stress on the body's energy systems and weight loss will slow to conserve energy.

As a rule of thumb, reducing calories by 300–400 a day, or getting down to 1200–1400 calories, will be enough to produce a good weight loss result over a 1–2 week period. If you also reduce your carbs from the average of 150–200 grams per day to 80–100 grams per day, and consume them mainly during the first half of the day, this will be enough to see you drop a few kilos rapidly.

Keeping a close eye on these numbers is crucial, as it is common to see individuals who drop their calories to as low as 800–1000 per day, and their carbs to 50 grams a day or less, who become extremely frustrated when they do not get the results they are looking for. It is easy to check your calories online, and it is also relatively easy to count your carbohydrates.

❖ *Remember: less is not better. You have to fuel the body to allow it to burn fat.*

SAMPLE 1500 CALORIE PLAN	SAMPLE 1200 CALORIE PLAN
Breakfast: 1 cup breakfast cereal with milk and banana	1 egg + 1 slice grain toast
Mid-morning: 200 g tub yoghurt + 1 fruit	4 grain crackers + 20 g light cheese
Lunch: Chicken salad sandwich + 1 fruit	Wrap bread with 95 g tuna and salad
Mid-afternoon: 30 g trail mix + 1 fruit	Meal replacement shake + berries
Dinner: 2 cups spaghetti bolognaise	100 g lean meat + vegetables
Dessert: 200 g low-fat yoghurt	Low-fat ice cream on a stick

When you are following a reduced-carb, low-calorie diet you will need to really focus on increasing your intake of low-calorie foods. Low-calorie foods tend to be water-based foods such as some fruits, most vegetables and some low-fat foods such as dips and miso soup. Often, once we start eating the volume of low-calorie foods, particularly the vegetables that we should eat for good health, we find we are automatically consuming fewer calories as we then feel full and satisfied, and lose weight as a result.

Throughout your 1–2 week program, as vegetables in particular are so low in calories, you can basically consume as many of these each day as you like. Use them to increase the bulk of your meals and snack freely on them throughout the day. It is almost the same in the case of the low-calorie foods listed. While these do not contain the nutritional benefits that vegetables do, they can also be used in circumstances where you may find yourself hungry in between your regular meals and snacks.

❈ *Shift your snack focus, and aim to snack on at least one vegetable rather than fruit each day.*

Simple ways to increase your intake of vegetables

1. Add some vegetables such as mushrooms or tomatoes to breakfast.
2. Snack on raw vegetables such as celery, cucumber and carrots.
3. Add a vegetable soup to one of your meals.
4. Add a large salad to lunch.
5. Include half a plate of vegetables or salad with your evening meal.

It is also useful to know which foods contain some of the fewest calories, so if you do find yourself desperately hungry, you'll be able to make the best choice.

Low-cal/low-carb super foods

	CARBS (G)	CALORIES
Strawberries, 1 cup	6	40
Mountain bread	13	70
2 corn cakes	4	20
2 rye crackers	6	30
1 small egg	0	50
1 cup popcorn	4	30
Miso soup	4	40

3. RID YOURSELF OF ANY EXTRA FLUID

With the human body consisting of 70 per cent fluid, our weight can differ by as much as 2–3 kilos from day to day depending on our bathroom habits, how much fluid we drink and how much fluid we retain. A classic example of this comes from a rugby player who had eaten 500 grams of dried meat on his way to training. As dried meat has an exceptionally high salt content, the player weighed in 5 kilos heavier than usual thanks to the extra fluid he had retained as his body attempted to wash out the extra salt being processed through his kidneys. A high intake of salt is just one of the reasons that your weight may vary from day to day.

Our bodies may retain extra fluid and leave us feeling bloated and heavy for a number of reasons. Women who are about to menstruate can gain up to 2 kilos pre-period. If you have not eaten adequate fibre to clear out your digestive tract you can retain a couple of kilos, as you can after eating a high-carb and/or high-salt diet or one-off meal. Overweight and/or larger-framed people retain more fluid than smaller people simply because they have more muscle mass, which will hold more stored carbohydrate, which attracts fluid. This is how morbidly obese people on reality television shows can be seen to have lost 5 or more kilos each time they weigh in – most of it is fluid.

There are a number of techniques you can use to achieve that elusive drop on the scales and relieve yourself of extra fluid and the bloated feeling that goes with it. First of all, you need to eliminate as much salt from your diet as you can. A low-salt diet will contain less than 1500 milligrams of sodium, but the average person consumes double this amount. To achieve this sodium target on a daily basis, you will need to eliminate all packaged and processed foods from your diet and eat only fresh, natural foods. This means no extra sauces, fast food or processed meats.

As you can see from the sodium counter below, it is easy to double your intake of sodium simply by adding a few extra sauces and snacks to your diet.

Foods very high in sodium

FOOD	SODIUM LEVEL (MG)
1 tsp salt	2000
Sausage (100 g)	650
Salami (50 g)	450
1 bacon rasher	650
1 doner kebab	1200
1 hamburger	1000
¼ pizza	1500
1 packet soup	700
½ cup baked beans	600
Potato chips (50 g)	450
1 piece garlic bread	470
1 tsp parmesan cheese	410

FOOD	SODIUM LEVEL (MG)
1 slice deli meat	300
1 tsp soy sauce	400
1 stock cube	700
4 olives	500
1 slice quiche	600
100 g smoked fish	1200
1 small meat pie	450
Packet of 2-minute noodles	600
420 g canned tomatoes	800
Frozen meal	700
2 cups Chinese takeaway	1000
1 piece battered fish	400
420 g canned spaghetti	500

Foods with a moderate level of sodium

FOOD	SODIUM LEVEL (MG)
1 slice cheese	200
1 tsp margarine	50
95 g can tuna in brine	270
1 cup breakfast cereal	200
50 g salted nuts	210
1 cracker biscuit	100
Sauces (per tbsp)	200–300

Foods low in sodium

FOOD	SODIUM LEVEL (MG)
250 ml milk	120
100 g plain meat	100
Tuna with no added salt	100
Bread (per slice)	200
1 cup breakfast cereal	20
50 g unsalted nuts	10
410 g canned tomatoes (no added salt)	20
Piece fresh fruit	0

Eating more vegetables is another easy way to help eliminate any extra fluid the body may be carrying. The high potassium content of vegetables helps to flush extra salt out of the body and for this reason, including a fresh vegetable juice as part of your diet can further support weight loss on the scales as well as help to reduce bloating. If you look at the examples below, you will see that it's easy to bulk up your diet with low-carb vegetables while adding only a few extra calories.

VEGETABLE JUICE

This nutrient-rich juice will help you shift fluid and give you a vitamin and mineral boost.

1 raw beetroot	Process in a blender or juicer.
3 sticks celery	
1 large carrot	
1 orange	
1 square ginger	**Serves 1**

❊ *Fruit-based juices are high in sugar and calories and so are not recommended on your 1–2 week plan. Switching to a vegetable-based juice gives you a nutrient hit without the calories.*

4. MAKE THE MOST OF SOUP

A rich vegetable soup can play a key role in helping you to lose a couple of kilos over 1–2 weeks. Vegetable soup is low in calories and extremely high in fibre, which not only helps to clear your bowels but is extremely filling which helps to control hunger when you are following a relatively strict food regime. A vegetable soup can be so powerful that even if you do nothing else but replace your dinner with a bowl of vegetable soup for a week, you may find that you lose a kilo simply via this dietary addition.

When choosing or preparing soup, remember that the starchy vegetables including legumes, potato, sweet potato, parsnip and corn contain much more carbohydrate than leafy vegetables and hence are not the best choice for a soup base. Instead, choose vegetables from the 'allium' family, including leeks, onions and garlic; these are particularly valuable as they have powerful diuretic properties, which means that they help to rid the body of extra fluid. Good vegetable options for your soup include pumpkin and carrots (which are not as high in carbs as many people believe), celery, zucchini, broccoli, cauliflower, leeks, mushrooms and onion. If you choose to make your own soup look for salt-reduced stocks where possible, as commercial stocks are usually high in sodium, which can defeat the purpose of using a soup to help rid the body of extra fluid it may be holding as a result of a high-salt diet.

VEGIE SOUP

2 teaspoons olive oil

1 onion, finely chopped

2 leeks, thinly sliced

2 cups salt-reduced vegetable stock + 3 cups water

2 × 420 g cans diced tomatoes

1 carrot, peeled and cut into 1 cm cubes

500 g pumpkin, cut into 1 cm cubes

1 head celery, chopped

1 head broccoli, steamed

1 Heat the olive oil in a large saucepan with the onion. Add the leek and cook gently over a low heat until soft. Add the stock, tomatoes, carrot, pumpkin and celery.

2 Bring to the boil, reduce the heat and simmer for 10 minutes.

3 Top with steamed broccoli and celery.

Serves 4

5. EAT SMALL MEALS

Size is crucial when it comes to eating for weight loss, yet it can be the most challenging aspect of the diet to control, particularly if you eat outside the home regularly. You may be surprised to hear that meals eaten out at restaurants or cafes can have as many as double the calories of the meals we would prepare at home. There are a few reasons for this, but the quality of ingredients, extra sauces and oils, and large serves of carbs such as rice and pasta as well as large meat serves are the main issues. It is also very easy to eat too much at home. We may cook more than we need, or think the portions specified in our eating plan are too small to sustain us and add a bit more or go back for seconds knowing that there is some food leftover.

To lose weight fast, you must be strict with your portion sizes. Eating 125 grams of meat for dinner when you should be having no more than 80 grams, or 40 grams of cheese instead of 20 grams, really does make a difference. For this reason, at least during your 1–2 week plan, you need to weigh and measure your key foods, in particular meat, carbohydrates, and sauces and oils. You will be surprised how little you need but how easy it is to slip in extras.

To optimise metabolism and maximise our weight loss success we need 5–6 small, regular meals every 3–4 hours, with no extra calories consumed in between. Where we often go wrong is having small extras such as a cup of coffee with milk, or a piece of fruit or a couple of biscuits, in between meals, which completely disrupts the digestive process and our natural hunger and fullness mechanisms. We then find ourselves eating when we are not hungry simply because it is 'mealtime' and taking in too many calories as a result.

To avoid getting trapped in this cycle of overeating, commit to a period of eating small volumes of food at mealtimes. A 'small' volume is equal to roughly 1–1½ cups of the carb and protein content of your meal, for example, a small piece of fish (protein) and one small potato (carbs). Often we are eating twice or three times this amount at meals. Once you have these portions, you can add an extra 2–3 cups of vegetables or salad. This way you have plenty of food but the calorie-containing components are much smaller, which helps to support your weight control.

Once you stop with the extras, and keep the actual carb and protein content of your meal small, you will notice that you naturally become hungry every few hours. This is a sign that your metabolism is working the way it should.

Key ways to watch your portions

Weigh your meat.

Cut the cheese from the block.

Measure out cereal.

Choose small slices of bread.

Use small cups for drinks.

Use teaspoons to measure oils and sauces.

Use spray oils where possible.

Use small plates, bowls and dishes.

Sample portions for weight loss

20 g slice of cheese

Palm-size (100 g) piece of meat, chicken or fish

2 teaspoons oil

100 g (½ cup) yoghurt

10 nuts

2 teaspoons avocado

Thin piece of wrap bread

¾ cup milk

¾ cup breakfast cereal

½ cup legumes or corn

6. KEEP DINNER LIGHT

Many quick weight loss programs are based on reducing carb intake to a very low level, and this technique undoubtedly works if you stick to the plan. When you are following a program for longer than 3–5 days, however, you have to be a little more careful about how you cut your carbs. While it may be tempting to cut them out all day, and grab plain tuna and salad for lunch, this approach tends to leave you vulnerable to excessive hunger and overeating later in the day. A far smarter approach, which will give a similar result, is to simply keep your dinner very light, with minimal carbs. This may mean having a meal replacement instead of a meal, swapping dinner for a soup or salad, or having a very small portion of protein with plain vegetables. If you can keep your dinner to 200–300 calories, you will get good results while avoiding the starvation response. It is also important to aim to have your last food for the day by 7 pm at the latest to give your body a good 10–12 hours without food overnight.

As a guide to dinner portions, ideally the carb and protein component of your dinner should fit into a small bowl or amount to 1 cup of food. This will be of food in addition to your 2–3 cups of vegetables, salad or soup. This relatively small volume of food is just enough to fill the stomach, increasing the chances that you will digest this food overnight and wake up hungry. If this sounds quite a bit less than you are used to eating, **the golden rule is to remember to bulk your dinner up with as much salad, vegetables and soup as you can.**

Contrary to popular belief, to lose weight you do not have to eat plain steamed vegetables. As vegetables are so low in calories, you can dress them up with tasty sauces so that they not only taste great but you eat far more of them because they do. To add flavour to your vegetables or salad, season with low-fat or 'free' dressings, herbs or a small (1 teaspoon) serve of oil-based dressing.

Sample 300 calorie dinners

80 g grilled protein (steak, chicken) + vegetable soup

100 g grilled salmon and salad

100 g grilled white fish + 1 small potato + green vegetables

1 lean sausage + pumpkin mash + green vegetables

½ cup pasta + ½ cup mince + 2 cups mixed salad/vegetables

1 piece mountain bread + ¾ cup mince or bean mix + salad

1 vegetarian pizza (vegie option – pumpkin, fetta, onion) made using
   mountain bread + salad

8 green prawns served with stir-fried zucchini, yellow squash, red capsicum

Tomato pasta sauce topped with 20 g crumbled fetta cheese

100 g white fish on bed of ½ cup cooked risotto + salad

7. BE FUSSY WITH YOUR DRINK CHOICES

If you had a month or two to lose weight, some extra liquid calories here or there, such as your favourite latte each morning or a glass of wine after work, would not be so much of an issue, but when you want to drop kilos quickly, liquid calories need to be monitored closely. Coffee and tea with milk added, a glass of wine or juice in the morning, or a sports drink when you are training are all extras – extras that have to go.

Switching to plain black coffee or tea, green or other herbal teas, and water will help you regulate your appetite. Your mid-morning coffee or numerous cups of tea with milk may be just the thing that is keeping your calorie intake higher than it needs to be, keeping extra kilos on in the process.

Drinking more fluid will also help to ensure that you are going to the bathroom regularly, avoiding any feelings of constipation or bloating.

❃ *Start each day with hot water with a slice of lemon added. It is a great daily ritual that will not only help to rehydrate you but also get you in the right mindset to start the day.*

DRINKS CALORIE COUNTER	CALORIES
Small skim cappuccino	60
Small skim latte	70
Piccolo latte	30
Macchiato	13
Large skim latte	130
Regular hot chocolate	170
Green tea	3
Tea with honey	25
Regular chai latte	130
Regular caramel latte	220

8. STAY HOME

You will make a huge leap forward when you begin to focus less on beating temptation and more on avoiding it.

It may sound harsh asking you to curb your social life, but if it helps you achieve your goal weight in a relatively short period of time, it will be worth it. The issue with going out is that your eating can get out of control very quickly. We are offered foods that we know we should not be having, one glass of wine becomes two, and then there are the diet saboteurs who make it their business to put us off track. Sure, if we have a long period in which to change our eating habits we can afford a few extras here and there, and in the long term this may even aid weight loss, but when we have just a week or two we have no such freedom.

A significant part of long-term weight control is developing the ability to self-regulate your food intake in all kinds of situations. It takes considerable time and effort to change your eating behaviour, and people who have lost large amounts of weight and kept it off often look upon weight control as an ongoing daily task. When you want to keep 100 per cent on track with a program for a short period of time, eliminate the risk of finding yourself in a situation in which it may be too hard for you to say no to high-calorie and/or high-fat foods.

Calories found in popular party and snack foods

	CARBS (G)	CALORIES
Average glass of wine	15	150
1 slice bread	15	100
3 canapés	30	200
2 serves cheese	0	200
Dessert	60	450
Packet of chips	22	260
Donut	24	180
Bucket of hot chips	39	370
Banana bread	30	200
Large flavoured coffee	30	250

9. STICK TO LIGHT TRAINING

People often think that rapid weight loss must involve intense workouts for numerous hours each day, but this is not so. An intense training session that lasts for longer than 30 or 40 minutes, whether it is a gym workout, a run or a fast walk, will lower your blood glucose levels, which can trigger extreme hunger and overeating. If this type of exercise regime is coupled with a low-carb, low-calorie diet, a significant imbalance between calories in versus calories out may result in a reduction in metabolic rate as the body tries to preserve the limited energy it is receiving from food.

So rather than exhaust yourself at the gym, in conjunction with your lower carb and calorie plan, you are better to include some light, moderate-intensity activity.

If you are already training regularly, just 20 minutes of high-intensity cardio is all you need to give yourself an extra calorie burn without completely depleting your glucose and glycogen stores, which may trigger hunger. A useful guide when it comes to calorie burning per workout is to aim to burn 200–300 calories during a 20–30 minute session. Generally speaking, interval training will help you to reach these calorie targets easily.

How to train more efficiently

Run intervals.

Change the speed, interval and incline of exercise machines.

Alternate machines every 10 minutes.

Do a different type of workout each day.

Walk hills and steps.

10. WALK AS MUCH AS YOU CAN

❀ *Walking should not be thought of as exercise. Walking is simply a way to make up for all the time we spend sitting down.*

It is not uncommon to see clients who train regularly but who then spend the rest of the day sitting down. Indeed, evidence suggests that the sedentary lifestyles we lead, spending much of the day in front of a computer or a television screen, do far more damage to our metabolism (that is, to our ability to burn calories) than poor eating habits do. For this reason, fitting in as much walking as you can, not as 'exercise' but simply to make up for the enormous amount of time you spend sitting, is a powerful way to get your muscles working again, burning calories and functioning much more efficiently.

Sample 1–2 week food plan

This menu contains an average of 1200 calories per day.

	MONDAY	TUESDAY	WEDNESDAY
BREAKFAST	1 poached egg + 1 slice grain toast + 1 glass vegetable juice	1 slice wholegrain toast + 130 g can baked beans + 2 kiwi fruit	⅓ cup oats + 1 cup low-fat milk + 2 kiwi fruit/ ½ cup mixed berries
MID-MORNING	1 piece fruit	100 g natural yoghurt + berries	1 piece fruit
LUNCH	100 g can tuna/ salmon + 130 g can mixed beans + mixed salad + 1 tsp dressing	100 g grilled chicken breast + 1 slice flat bread+ mixed salad + 1 tsp dressing	½ cup brown rice + 95 g can tuna mixed with red capsicum and sweet chilli sauce
MID-AFTERNOON	10 walnuts	15 almonds + 1 apple	2 corn thins + 1 tsp of peanut butter
DINNER	150 g grilled white fish + vegetables stir-fried in 1 tsp olive oil	100 g lean steak fillet + salad	100 g grilled chicken + salad

Adding in a couple of walks, ideally one 20–30 minutes before breakfast and another after dinner, is a simple yet effective way burn some extra calories at each end of the day and speed up weigh loss.

THURSDAY	FRIDAY	SATURDAY	SUNDAY
1 poached egg + 1 slice wholegrain toast + 1 glass tomato/vegetable juice	1 slice wholegrain toast + 130 g can baked beans + 2 kiwi fruit	⅓ cup oats + 1 cup low-fat milk + 2 kiwi fruit/½ cup mixed berries	2 poached eggs + 2 slices Tip Top 9 grain
100 g natural yoghurt + ½ cup berries	1 piece fruit	100 g natural yoghurt + berries	1 piece fruit
100 g can tuna/salmon + 130 g can mixed beans + mixed salad + 1 tsp of dressing	100 g grilled chicken breast + 1 slice flat bread + mixed salad	Jacket potato topped with red salmon + ⅓ cup cottage cheese + tomato	100 g lean beef strips + 1 piece flat bread + salad
1 fruit	2 corn thins + 1 tsp of avocado	15 almonds	10 walnuts
150 g grilled fish + vegetables stir-fried in 1 tsp olive oil	100 g lean lamb + vegetables	100 g tuna fillet with Asian vegetables	Vegetable soup + 100 g grilled Atlantic salmon

RECIPES FOR YOUR
1–2 WEEK PLAN

The recipes featured in this section contain 300 calories and can be used as dinner options.

CHEESY CUTLETS

1 cup multigrain breadcrumbs

3 tablespoons chopped parsley

½ cup grated 50% reduced-fat cheddar cheese

8 small lean lamb cutlets, trimmed

1 egg, lightly beaten

2 teaspoons olive oil

4 cups green vegetables

4 medium carrots

1 In a bowl combine the breadcrumbs, parsley and cheese. Dip the lamb cutlets into the egg and then press each side into the breadcrumb mixture. Place on a tray lined with non-stick baking paper and refrigerate for 20 minutes.

2 Heat the oil in a large non-stick frying pan over medium heat. Cook the cutlets in two batches for 2 minutes each side or until the crust is golden and the meat is cooked.

3 Serve with steamed green vegetables and carrots.

Serves 4

SALSA PORK

4 small lean pork cutlets

2 teaspoons olive oil

Salsa

130 g can corn kernels

1 small nectarine or peach, finely diced

1 small red chilli

2 Roma tomatoes, finely diced

1 tablespoon chopped mint

1 teaspoon lemon rind

1 tablespoon lemon juice

4 cups mixed salad leaves

1 Mix salsa ingredients with a small amount of olive oil.

2 Grill cutlets over medium heat and serve with 2 tablespoons of salsa and salad leaves.

Serves 4

MINI MEATBALLS

500 g extra-lean beef mince

1 medium onion, grated

1 medium carrot, grated

1 small zucchini, grated

2 tablespoons reduced-salt tomato sauce

1 tablespoon barbecue sauce

½ cup extra-light grated cheddar cheese

3 tablespoons plain flour

¾ cup multigrain breadcrumbs

2 teaspoons canola oil

4 cups mixed salad

1 Place the beef, onion, carrot, zucchini, tomato sauce, barbecue sauce, cheese and flour in a bowl and mix to combine.

2 Shape the mixture into patties the size of a 50 cent piece. Roll each patty in breadcrumbs and place on a tray. Refrigerate until firm.

3 Bake in the oven at 200ºC for 30–40 minutes, or lightly fry over medium heat in canola oil. Serve with unlimited fresh salad.

**Serves 4
(makes 15–20 meatballs)**

QUICK CHICKEN SOUP

1 whole chicken

1 medium onion, cut into wedges

3 cloves garlic smashed with flat side of knife

2 stalks celery leaves and stems, chopped

1 bay leaf

2 carrots, cut into chunks

1 Put the chicken in a stockpot. Scatter the onion, garlic, celery, bay leaf and salt to taste around the chicken. Cover the chicken with water and put a lid on the pot; bring to the boil and boil for 5 minutes. Turn off the heat and allow the chicken to poach in the water for 45 minutes (don't remove the lid during this time).

2 Once the chicken is cooked, remove it from the stock and allow it to cool sufficiently to handle. Remove and discard the skin; then strip the meat off the bones and tear into bite-size pieces. Cover the chicken and refrigerate.

3 Return the bones to the stockpot along with any reserved juices from the chicken. Cover and bring to the boil, then reduce heat and simmer for 3 hours.

4 Strain the stock through a fine mesh sieve and discard the solids. Skim off any excess oil, then return the soup to the pot along with the carrots. Cook until carrots are tender and then serve.

Serves 6–8

BEST TOMATO SOUP

12 Roma tomatoes, finely chopped

4 large cloves garlic, finely chopped

1 large onion, cut into quarters

¼ cup olive oil

1 teaspoon sugar

500 ml salt-reduced vegetable stock

10 fresh basil leaves

1 Place tomatoes, onion, garlic and olive oil in a large oven tray, sprinkling sugar over the tomatoes.

2 Bake at 180°C for about 30 minutes.

3 Add the vegetable stock and basil leaves and bake for a further 20 minutes.

4 Blend and serve.

Serves 6–8

QUINOA PATTIES

2½ cups cooked quinoa

4 large eggs, beaten

6 cloves garlic, minced

⅔ cup fresh chives, chopped

1 red onion, finely chopped

⅓ cup fresh Parmesan cheese, grated

1 cup wholegrain breadcrumbs

2 teaspoons extra virgin olive oil

4 cups mixed salad

1 Combine quinoa and eggs. Stir in garlic, chives, onion and cheese. Add breadcrumbs.

2 Form into patties approximately 2.5 cm in diameter. The mixture should be very moist.

3 Heat a pan over medium heat and add the olive oil. Fry patties for 8–10 minutes until browned; then flip and cook for 7 more minutes. Serve with salad.

Serves 4–6

PUMPKIN AND LEEK SOUP

2 leeks

2 teaspoons olive oil

2 large or 4 small onions, finely chopped

2 garlic cloves, minced

300 g butternut pumpkin, cubed

4 cups reduced-salt chicken stock

2 cups water

1 Halve leeks lengthways, wash thoroughly under cold water and then slice into thin slices. Place the olive oil, leek and onion in a large soup pot; bring to the boil and simmer for 5 minutes, stirring frequently. Add the minced garlic and cook for another minute.

2 Add all the remaining ingredients and simmer until the pumpkin is tender.

3 Puree with a stick blender or in a food processor, and serve.

Serves 6–8

JOHN DORY WITH PUMPKIN MASH

1 butternut pumpkin, peeled and cubed

¼ cup low-fat milk

2 teaspoons reduced-fat spread

2 teaspoons olive oil

2 large John Dory fillets

2 teaspoons pesto

2 cups green beans

1 Steam the pumpkin until tender; then mash with the milk and spread.

2 Heat the olive oil in a pan and seal the fish fillets; reduce heat and cook until fish flakes when tested with a fork. Place the fish on a bed of pumpkin mash, drizzle with pesto and serve with lightly steamed green beans.

Serves 2

Tips and tricks for your 1–2 week program

- Try not to think too much about food – the more you think about it, the more you will want it.

- Rid the house of any extra food you may be tempted to eat at times when you should not be eating.

- Remember that any cravings or withdrawal symptoms from sugar or caffeine will last for 2–3 days at most.

- Remember that hunger is a good sign. It is a sign your body is starting to burn the food you eat.

- Try and limit yourself to just one milk-based coffee a day.

- Aim to eat your breakfast as early as possible, ideally by 8 am.

- Aim for 10–12 hours without food overnight.

- Limit training to just 30 minutes a day.

- Walk as much as you can.

- Eat as many vegetables or as much vegetable soup as you like.

- Avoid friends and family who may act to sabotage your diet by bringing you food or encouraging you to eat extra.

1–2 week weight loss checklist

1. Use a meal replacement.
2. Keep your calories and carbohydrates low.
3. Rid yourself of any extra fluid.
4. Make the most of soup.
5. Eat small meals.
6. Keep dinner light.
7. Be fussy with your drink choices.
8. Stay home.
9. Stick to light training.
10. Walk as much as you can.

When you have a month

❖ *A month is a great period of time to dedicate to weight loss. It is long enough to get decent results as well as enough time to develop some strong diet and exercise habits.*

When you have longer than a week or two to lose weight, you also have more options. Research suggests that people do better on a weight-loss program in the long term if they lose weight initially. When you have 4 weeks, this may mean starting with a 1200 calorie program as featured in the 1–2 week program and dropping a couple of kilos quickly before switching to a slightly higher calorie intake for the final week or two. Exercising regularly and intensely is crucial, as we want to work the muscles harder to increase the metabolic rate. The good news is that unlike the stricter 3–5 day and 1–2 week weight loss programs, you don't have to become a hermit. A few extra calories from drinking alcohol occasionally or enjoying a meal out once a week should not undo too much of your hard work.

Getting in the right mindset to stay on track for 4 weeks

First and foremost, you need to commit fully to the program and get organised. This may mean clearing out the social diary a little, bumping up the time you allocate to exercise and making sure you have the foods you need to stick to your program readily available. As reasonable focus is required, try to choose a month when you don't have any major events that may cause you to go completely off the rails, such as holidays or big celebrations. Then, before you begin it will be useful to ask yourself the following questions:

- What are the biggest and most important changes I need to make to my lifestyle in the long term to help me get to and maintain the weight I would like to be?

- What has been preventing me from making these changes before?

- How much weight do I want to lose in a month?

- What will I need to do to get these results?

- Can I commit to this process 100 per cent for the next 4 weeks?

Once you have had time to consider these things, and perhaps made some notes to help focus your thoughts, the only thing you need to do is to take control of your food and your exercise. Four weeks is not long, so if you approach training and calorie intake in the right way, you could easily be 5–10 kilos lighter at the end of the month.

10 key strategies for your 4 week weight loss program

1. GET BREAKFAST RIGHT

One of the most effective things you can do is to eat a protein-rich breakfast as early as possible. The body's hormones and metabolism are programmed to a 24 hour circadian rhythm, so **the earlier in the day you eat your breakfast, the more energy you are likely to burn.** This is why, on days when you have had an early breakfast, you may feel extreme hunger a few hours later. Even 8 am or 9 am is a little too late to enjoy the first meal of the day. To optimise metabolism and kick-start calorie burning, eat your protein-rich breakfast before 8 am each day.

A protein-rich breakfast supports weight loss because protein requires more calories to digest than carbohydrates or fats. Protein also helps to slow digestion and control the release of the hormones that help to control appetite. Protein-rich breakfast options include eggs, lean ham, smoked salmon or sardines, baked beans and protein-rich shakes.

While you may have been taught, or think, that you will get better weight loss results by eliminating carbohydrates at breakfast, cutting your primary source of fuel so early in the day will do nothing to promote fat burning. You will get just as good or even better results over a 4 week period by including a small amount of carbs (20–30 grams) with your breakfast than you would if you eliminated them entirely.

Top breakfast options

1 egg omelette (see recipe on page 67)

Breakfast Shake (see recipe on page 68)

1 egg with 1 slice wholegrain toast

2 corn crackers with ½ cup cottage cheese

Small skim latte and 1 hard-boiled egg

1 slice wholegrain toast with 25 g 97% fat-free ham and 1 slice light Jarlsberg cheese

Meal replacement shake

100 g Greek yoghurt with ½ cup mixed berries and 1 teaspoon protein powder

Smoked salmon and ricotta wrap on wholegrain flatbread

200 ml vegetable/tomato juice and ½ cup bran cereal with 1 cup low-fat milk

ULTIMATE BREAKFAST OMELETTE

1 whole egg plus 1 egg white

½ cup low-fat milk

1 cup chopped vegetables (mushrooms, tomato, onion, English spinach, capsicum)

20 g reduced-fat fetta or goat's cheese

Olive oil spray

2 tablespoons grated reduced-fat cheese

1 Beat egg and egg white with milk. Combine chopped vegetables with fetta or goat's cheese.

2 Spray hot pan with olive oil and coat bottom of pan with the egg mixture.

3 Once the egg is set, add the vegetables down the centre and fold over one side of the omelette. Cook until sealed and sprinkle with grated cheese.

Serves 1

BREAKFAST SHAKE

20 g vanilla-flavoured whey protein powder

¾ cup mixed berries

200 ml low-fat milk

½ teaspoon vanilla essence

Blend all ingredients together for a delicious, high-protein breakfast shake.

Serves 1

2. GET YOUR SNACK BALANCE RIGHT

Many people who are trying to lose weight think they should eat as little as possible, which means they try not to eat between meals. This style of eating may work for some, but there is also good evidence to show that eating small, regular meals has a powerful effect on metabolism. As it takes a certain number of calories to digest your food, having several small (note small!) meals throughout the day will help to burn more calories than you would if you had just two or three larger meals.

For this reason, if you keep your breakfast relatively small, you are likely to be hungry 2–3 hours after breakfast and so you will need a small meal/snack to take you through until lunchtime. This snack will ideally contain 150–200 calories and include a serve of slowly digested carbohydrates and a serve of protein. The mix of carbohydrates and proteins will help to control the release of the hormone insulin, which will in turn help to optimise fat metabolism and control your appetite.

The most common issue with the snacks we choose is that they are too big – we have 6 crackers instead of 2 or a large coffee instead of a small. The key to optimising metabolism during this phase of your program is to control the size of your snacks.

Best carb/protein snack options

4 wholegrain crackers with 40 g reduced-fat cheese

Small skim coffee and 20 g reduced-fat cheese

1 piece of fruit and 20 g reduced-fat cheese

100 g natural yoghurt with ½ cup mixed berries

Packet of roasted chickpeas and small skim milk coffee

130 g can of baked beans with 2 corn thins

2 corn thins with 2 tablespoons of cottage cheese

Mountain bread wrap with 50 g low-fat meat

2 rye crackers with tomato and 4 tablespoons of low fat ricotta

Regular skim milk coffee

SNACK-TIME YOGHURT

150 ml (¾ cup) natural or Greek-style yoghurt

5 walnuts, 5 almonds, chopped

2 teaspoons dried cranberries

½ teaspoon cinnamon

½ cup mixed berries (fresh or frozen)

Mix all ingredients together for a delicious mid-morning snack.

Serves 1

CRANBERRY BISCOTTI

½ cup dried cranberries	1 cup sugar
½ cup boiling water	3 large eggs
3 cups flour	2 teaspoons pure vanilla extract
2 teaspoons baking powder	
¼ teaspoon salt	½ cup unsalted pistachios, coarsely chopped
4 tablespoons unsalted butter, at room temperature	

1 Preheat oven to 180ºC. Line a large baking sheet with baking paper; set aside.

2 Place cranberries in a small bowl and add boiling water. Let stand for 15 minutes. Drain, and set aside.

3 Sift flour, baking powder and salt into a medium bowl; set aside.

4 In the bowl of an electric mixer fitted with the paddle attachment, beat butter and sugar on medium speed until light and fluffy (about 2 minutes). Add 3 eggs, one at a time, beating to incorporate after each addition and scraping down sides of bowl as needed. Beat in vanilla.

5 Add flour mixture and mix on low speed until combined. Mix in cranberries and pistachios.

6 Turn out dough onto a lightly floured surface; divide in half. Shape each piece into a 40 cm x 5 cm log and transfer to the prepared baking sheet, about 7 cm apart. With the palm of your hand, flatten logs slightly. Brush logs with a beaten egg and sprinkle with a small amount of sugar.

7 Bake, rotating the baking sheet halfway through, until the logs are slightly firm to touch (about 25 minutes). Transfer logs on baking paper to a wire rack to cool slightly (about 20 minutes). Reduce oven temperature to 140ºC.

8 Place logs on a cutting board. Using a serrated knife, cut logs crosswise on the diagonal into 2–3 cm thick slices.

9 Place a wire rack on a large, rimmed baking sheet. Arrange slices, cut sides down, on rack. Bake until firm to touch (about 30 minutes). Remove pan from oven and leave biscotti to cool completely on the rack.

10 Biscotti can be kept in an airtight container at room temperature for up to one week.

✿ *If your lunch does not contain 2 cups of vegetables or salad, you are likely to be unsatisfied all afternoon.*

3. GET YOUR LUNCH BALANCE RIGHT

A common mistake among dieters is to fail to get enough salad or vegetables at lunchtime. Too often they eat a plain sandwich or wrap or sushi, which leaves them feeling unsatisfied and craving sugar an hour or two later.

Throughout your 4 week program, it is crucially important to have at least 2 cups of vegetables or salad with your lunch. This can be in the form of soup, cooked or raw vegetables, or a salad, but be aware that few ready-prepared salads you buy will have this quantity. Next you need a palm-size serve (about 100 grams) of a lean source of protein. Again, the protein will help to regulate your energy levels throughout the afternoon as well as provide important nutrients, including iron, zinc and vitamin B_{12}. Finally, while you may be tempted to eliminate carbs at lunchtime, it is a little early in the day to do so. As your total carbohydrate intake will already be relatively low, with just one serve at breakfast and another 1–2 serves in your mid-morning snack, you still need a serve of carbs at lunch (and men need 2 serves). This can be as simple as adding some sweet potato to your salad, or a slice of bread or a wrap, or some beans or corn.

Top lunch choices

95 g can tuna with 130 g can beans and mixed salad

6–8 pieces of sashimi with seaweed salad

Mountain bread wrap with 100 g turkey breast and salad

100 g chicken with Greek salad and a small skim coffee

4 rye crackers with red salmon, cottage cheese and salad

Bowl of vegetable soup and 2 rye crackers with tuna

½ large wholegrain meat and salad sandwich

2 boiled eggs with 4 corn crackers and green salad

Meal replacement shake and large salad

Lamb salad with roasted vegetables

LUNCH RECIPES

CRUNCHY NOODLE SALAD

¼ cup rice vinegar

2 tablespoons sesame oil

1 tablespoon sugar

¼ iceberg lettuce

1 cup cooked chicken breast

½ red capsicum

1 cup 97% fat-free 2-minute noodles

¼ avocado (sprinkled with lemon juice)

1 Whisk together vinegar, oil and sugar.

2 Mix salad ingredients (except noodles and avocado) and drizzle with dressing.

3 Top with crunchy noodles and avocado.

Serves 1

CHICK NUT SALAD WITH CHICKEN OR LAMB

½ Lebanese cucumber

2 Roma tomatoes, diced

20 g reduced-fat fetta, crumbled

1 cup rocket or English spinach leaves

100 g grilled chicken breast or lamb fillet, diced

½ cup chick nuts (roasted chickpeas)

2 teaspoons salad dressing

Mix all ingredients together for a delicious lunchtime salad.

Serves 1

TUNA AND BROWN RICE SALAD

½ cup cooked brown rice

½ punnet cherry tomatoes, halved

1 small Lebanese cucumber

1 cup rocket or baby spinach

100 g can tuna in oil, drained

5 pecan nuts

30 g reduced-fat fetta cheese

Low-fat French dressing

Mix ingredients with cooked brown rice. Dress lightly with French dressing.

Serves 1

SALMON AND DANISH FETTA

105 g can red salmon or 50 g
smoked salmon

2 cups rocket or English
spinach

½ cup roasted pumpkin
pieces

2 Roma tomatoes, chopped

½ red onion, diced

130 g can corn or four bean
mix

20 g Danish fetta

2 teaspoons light balsamic
dressing

Mix ingredients together and dress
with light balsamic dressing.

Serves 1

NIÇOISE SALAD

½ cup green beans

100 g can tuna in oil, drained

1 green onion, thinly sliced

5 cherry tomatoes, halved

1 cup mixed lettuce

½ teaspoon finely grated
lemon rind

50 ml (⅛ cup) lemon juice

1 teaspoon wholegrain
mustard

1 clove garlic, crushed

1 teaspoon sugar

1 Cook beans until tender.

2 Combine beans with tuna,
onion, tomatoes and lettuce in
a large bowl.

3 Whisk remaining ingredients in
a small bowl; add to salad and
toss gently to combine.

Serves 1

4. HAVE SOUP ONCE A DAY

The reason that soup is so often mentioned in books and magazine articles about weight loss is that there is evidence to show that eating a bowl of low-calorie soup before a meal will help to curb your appetite and result in you eating up to 100 calories less at the meal. Vegetable soup also gives you a good dose of fibre, and those that contain plenty of leek, onions and garlic have a 'strip' effect as they pass through the digestive tract, helping to rid the body of extra fluid. While this is only fluid loss, the psychological benefits of seeing a positive change on the scales is often all you need to feel motivated to stay on your program.

A vegetable-based soup can be used in several ways on a weight loss plan. You can use it as an 'extra' when you are feeling hungry or as a meal replacement at night-time to help keep your calories low, or you can add it to either lunch or dinner to help keep your calories low while maintaining your vegetable bulk on a reduced-calorie plan.

VEGETABLE SOUP WITH CHICKEN

1 skinless chicken breast fillet

1 litre reduced-salt chicken stock

1 tablespoon canola oil

2 leeks, washed and thinly sliced

2 carrots, diced

2 sticks celery, diced

3 cloves garlic, crushed

6 cups young green salad leaves (watercress, rocket, sorrel, baby spinach), washed

1 Place chicken in a pot, add just enough chicken stock to cover, and poach gently for about 10 minutes or until just cooked. Set aside to cool.

2 Heat the oil in a large pot, add the leeks and cook gently for about 2 minutes until soft. Add the carrot, celery and garlic.

3 Strain the chicken poaching stock through a fine sieve and add to the vegetables with the rest of the stock. Simmer for 10 minutes.

4 Chop the greens finely, add to the soup and cook for a further 10 minutes.

5 Tear the chicken breasts into fine shreds and add them to the soup.

Serves 4

5. HAVE A PROTEIN-RICH AFTERNOON SNACK

Even if your lunch was perfectly balanced nutritionally, if you have successfully kick-started the fat-burning process and eaten your lunch at the right time (between 12 pm and 1 pm), you will be hungry by 3–4 pm. The most common mistake that people make at this time is that they try not to eat, only to experience a distinct drop in blood glucose late in the afternoon, which results in intense sugar cravings and overeating. A much better way to manage this situation is to plan to have a calorie-controlled, protein-rich snack just before you get really hungry. As it is now later in the day, we can start to cut back on carbs at this time and concentrate on protein-rich choices. Again, bulk is important, so that you feel satisfied and are not tempted to eat again until dinnertime.

Ideally, we are aiming for a snack with 150–200 calories, at least 5–10 grams of protein and a total of 10–20 grams of carbohydrates. The protein component will help to regulate the hormones that affect appetite, while the carbohydrate component will help prevent any sugar cravings. Here is a list of snacks that fit this nutrient profile.

4 week weight loss snack list

Nut-based snack bar

100 g Greek yoghurt with 10 nuts and ½ cup mixed berries

2 rye or corn crackers with extra-light cream cheese and 10 nuts

30 g mixed nuts

1 piece of fruit and 20 g reduced-fat cheese

Protein shake

2 rye crackers with 2 teaspoons of peanut butter

20 g pack of chick nuts (roasted chickpeas)

Meal replacement shake or bar

Protein bar

If you continually find that, despite having eaten something quite substantial in the mid-afternoon, you are still hungry and craving more food, you can snack freely on cut-up vegetables such as carrots, cucumber and celery. These are all low-calorie choices and should help to fill you up and control your cravings.

6. EAT DINNER BY 7 PM

If we were to eat breakfast at 7, lunch by 12 and dinner by 6, we would all have far fewer weight issues. In reality, many of us are lucky to have eaten breakfast by 9 am, lunch by 2 pm and dinner by 8 pm or 9 pm. Eating most of our food in the second half of the day is an issue for weight loss, as hormonally we are programmed to burn calories during the first half of the day and store them the later we eat.

While it may take some extra planning to make sure that you eat your dinner as early as possible, at least for a few days of the week, the benefits include having a couple of hours after dinner to process your food, waking up the next day hungry and ready for breakfast, and – perhaps best of all – that feeling of 'I am losing weight', which is very powerful psychologically as we strive to stay on track with any new routine.

If your work day routinely finishes late and you find yourself not eating until after 8 pm, one option is to have your 'dinner' meal at lunchtime, even if it is leftovers from the night before, and then to have a light meal or snack later in the evening. Here are some good options.

Top late night dinners

1 egg omelette (see recipe on page 67)

Jacket potato with 95 g can of tuna or salmon

Rye crackers with tuna or salmon

Stir-fried vegetables

Meal replacement shake

Frozen fish with vegetables

Mezze plate with cut-up vegetables, hummus and lean meat

Chicken strips and salad

Pumpkin soup

Sushi roll and seaweed salad

One thing in particular to beware of is grabbing the quick, high-carb dinner options of toast, breakfast cereal, quick-cook rice or pasta when you are tired and starving. High-carb options result in a relatively high secretion of the hormone insulin, which is a hormone that tells the body to 'store and build'. If it is secreted late at night, this will increase the likelihood that your body will be storing fat rather than burning it. For this reason, the later you have your dinner, the lighter, particularly in carbs, it needs to be.

7. TRAIN AND WALK

You may be under the impression that the more exercise you do, the faster you will lose weight. This is not so. During a phase of intense weight loss, it is important to remember that as your calories have already been dramatically restricted, burning more calories via intense training may result in too great a deficit between calories in versus calories out to see maximum weight loss. If you were to train intensely, or for long periods of time, for a number of days, at some point your body would identify this calorie deficit and may slow metabolic rate to preserve calories. To avoid this scenario instead commit to a shorter period of high-intensity training – say, 20–30 minutes in which you aim to burn 200–300 calories.

One way to do this is to enlist the help of a personal trainer for a short period of time. It is easy to fall into a pattern of thinking you have trained a lot when in reality you are not training as intensely as you could or should. Remember the mantra 'quality over quantity' when it comes to training and use objective measures of intensity, whether it is via a heart rate monitor, your calorie output or a personal trainer, to ensure that you are getting the maximum results for the time you put in.

Once you have scheduled at least three 30-minute high-intensity sessions into your week, the next component of your training regime is to make sure you are also moving your body. Many of us spend hours and hours of our day sitting, whether it is at work, in front of the computer or television, or driving. Research has shown that the more sitting we do, the worse it is for our metabolism, even if we train regularly. Committing to walking for 20–30 minutes each day is one way to compensate for some of this sedentary time. It doesn't matter if you do this before breakfast, at lunchtime or after dinner, the more low-intensity movement you add into your day, whether it be house-work, gardening or walking, the more weight you are likely to lose.

❧ *Eating 5–10 walnuts every day has numerous health benefits above and beyond those we get from eating most other types of nuts.*

8. EAT SOME NUTS EVERY DAY

Nuts can play a useful role in a weight loss program. The right mix of nuts can help you achieve the right fat balance in your diet, which can in turn help your cells to burn fat effectively. The key is choosing the right mix of nuts, and knowing when you need to stop eating them.

Dietary modelling, which is used to work out how many grams of food equate to the relative quantities of carbs, proteins and fats we need to achieve certain calorie and carb targets for weight loss, show that eating just 10–15 nuts each day will give us the 10–20 grams of 'good fats' we need. Walnuts are particularly good at increasing our intake of the essential omega-3 fats (the kind found in oily fish), which have numerous health benefits. So, as part of your 4 week plan, eat 10–15 nuts every day, and include at least 5 walnuts in this mix.

9. DRINK ONLY . . .

Liquid calories in the form of cups of tea or coffee with milk, juices, soft drinks, energy drinks, shakes and, of course, alcohol can be an issue for many people wanting to lose weight. The problem is that they are not compensated for, which means that we don't eat less simply because we have had them. For those of us who are used to enjoying 2 or 3 cappuccinos a day or half a bottle of wine, this is a major problem.

If you want to shed kilos quickly, the fewer liquid calories you consume, the better. This means that you need to focus on drinking water and herbal tea and to limit yourself to just one or two cups of coffee or tea. Carry a water bottle with you at all times and aim to drink at least one 500–600 ml bottle in the morning and another throughout the afternoon. Drink herbal tea instead of milk-based drinks, and try to commit to an alcohol-free month. This will help to shift a few kilos quickly over your 4 week program and will also help to keep you focused and motivated.

Liquid calories (per serve)

Water	0
Flavoured water	100
Energy drink	150
Cola drink (600 ml)	250
Small fruit smoothie (350 ml)	125
Regular fruit smoothie (650 ml)	350
Vitamin water (500 ml)	120
Sports drink (600 ml)	190
Green tea (200 ml)	6
Large coffee (400 ml)	250

10. HAVE A MEAL OFF OCCASIONALLY

Unlike weight loss plans designed to shift kilos over a week or two, when you have a month you have a little more freedom. A meal here or there with some extra calories is not going to completely destroy the program as long as you don't interpret this freedom as an opportunity to binge. **It is not uncommon for weight loss clients to turn a 'meal off' into a full-blown binge and to polish off an entire pizza, a bottle of wine and a block of chocolate in one sitting.**

The 'all or nothing' mindset is deeply entrenched in many dieters and is often the thing that derails almost every new diet or fad we try. It takes time to overcome this and to accept that you can eat 'naughty', higher-calorie foods occasionally and still lose weight, just as it takes time to change any longstanding thought pattern or habit. We need to give ourselves that time.

The other thing to consider is how we define a meal 'off'. Nutritionally, it means eating something higher in fat and calories than you usually would, not bingeing on an entire pizza because you think you can, even if you don't even like eating pizza all that much. Taking a meal off means enjoying a heavier restaurant meal, or sharing a dessert instead of skipping dessert as you usually would, or enjoying a couple of glasses of wine on a Friday night – not all three. The crucial thing is then to get straight back on track with your usual diet regime at the very next meal.

So, as you commit to shifting your 5–10 kilos, get into the habit of planning your week ahead so that you know in advance when you may indulge a little more. This enables you to compensate appropriately during the week and also removes the need to make a decision when you are offered food. If you have decided in advance that you will not be eating cake at work, or drinking alcohol, it will be much easier to say no. And remember, once you have said no the first time, it gets easier each time you do it.

Ideally, a meal off will contain no more than 200–300 calories more than you would usually consume in a single meal. For example, you might have pasta or a rice-based meal, or a couple of glasses of wine, or you might share a dessert with your partner. A meal off allows you to juggle any social engagements you may have, or simply provides a little balance when you have been fairly rigid with your diet for most of the week. A meal off may even help you to maximise weight loss by telling the body that you are not starving it. But it's crucial that the extra calories translate into just one higher-calorie meal per week throughout your month-long program.

SAMPLE HIGHER-CALORIE MEALS	CALORIES
2 cups of pasta with 1 cup of sauce	400
Thai meal with 1 cup of cooked rice	500
2 glasses of wine	300
50 g chocolate	250
1 serve of pudding or 1 slice of cake	350
2 slices of pizza	400
2 chocolate biscuits	200
Slice of cake at work	350
Fast food meal	500–600
Three-course meal	600–1000

Sample 4 week food plan

This menu contains an average of 1400 calories per day.

	MONDAY	TUESDAY	WEDNESDAY
BREAKFAST	30 g (¾ cup) bran cereal with 100 g (½ cup) natural yoghurt mixed with ½ cup mixed berries	1 slice wholegrain bread with 130 g (½ cup) baked beans and 20 g (¼ cup) reduced-fat cheese	Small wholemeal wrap filled with 1 poached egg, 1 slice smoked salmon, rocket and tomato, and 1 tbsp low-fat mayonnaise
MID-MORNING	2 rye crackers + 2 tbsp cottage cheese + 1 small apple	Small skim coffee + 1 punnet of berries	Small skim coffee
LUNCH	100 g pink or red salmon with large mixed green salad + ¼ avocado + 1 piece fruit	Small wholegrain or wholemeal wrap with 100 g turkey breast, 1 slice Jarlsberg cheese, tomato and rocket + 2 apricots or 1 peach	4 wholegrain crackers with 95 g can chilli tuna, ¼ avocado and 8 cherry tomatoes + ½ cup low-fat fruit yoghurt
MID-AFTERNOON	30 g mixed nuts	2 corn crackers + 2 tsp peanut butter + 1 carrot	Small nut snack bar
DINNER	150 g grilled white fish with roasted eggplant, zucchini, pumpkin and red capsicum	100 g chicken breast with 1 tsp sweet chilli sauce + 100 g roasted pumpkin and green beans	100 g grilled fillet steak with 1 medium jacket potato and 1 tsp light sour cream + large green salad

THURSDAY	FRIDAY	SATURDAY	SUNDAY
2 slices wholegrain bread with 1 poached egg + 4 sautéed mushrooms and 2 roasted tomatoes	30 g (¾ cup) wheat bran cereal with 100 g (½ cup) natural yoghurt mixed with ¾ cup mixed berries	1 egg omelette	8 sautéed mushrooms on 2 small slices sourdough or wholegrain toast sprinkled with 20 g reduced-fat fetta
2 crackers + 1 slice light cheese + 1 piece fruit	Small skim coffee + 20 g light cheese		
½ cup cooked brown rice with 100 g chicken/ tuna + mixed vegetables with 2 tsp sweet chilli sauce	100 g grilled chicken breast with 1 piece wholemeal wrap bread, lettuce, tomato and 1 tbsp reduced-fat mayonnaise + 1 small mango	2 slices wholegrain bread, toasted, with 130 g baked beans + 2 slices watermelon	Chicken caesar salad: 100 g grilled chicken breast, 1 slice 97% fat-free bacon, 2 tbsp low-fat caesar dressing, lettuce and cherry tomatoes
30 g mixed nuts + 1 punnet of berries	30 g tub of hummus + cut-up vegetables		
100 g lean lamb fillet with 1 small wholemeal burrito wrap	100 g grilled Atlantic salmon with pumpkin, rocket and walnut salad and 1 tsp honey mustard dressing	Homemade pizza: 100 g lean chicken breast, mushrooms, tomato and rocket with a sprinkle of light mozzarella cheese on wholemeal pita bread + large green salad	150 g barbecued fish + mixed green salad + 1 scoop low-fat ice-cream and ½ cup mixed berries

RECIPES FOR YOUR 4 WEEK PLAN

All recipes can be used as dinner options throughout your 4 week plan and contain between 300 and 400 calories.

BEST VEGETABLE SALAD

1 tablespoon olive oil

1 tablespoon white wine vinegar

1 tablespoon lemon juice

4 asparagus spears

1 carrot, sliced

1 small zucchini, sliced lengthways

1 small red capsicum, sliced

10 snow peas

1 cup cannellini beans

1 cup bean sprouts

3 tablespoons goat's cheese

1 Mix oil, vinegar and lemon juice to make dressing.

2 Mix vegetables with dressing and serve with a little goat's cheese – perfect served with a 150 g piece of lamb or steak.

Serves 4

GRILLED SALMON WITH BEAN SALAD

4 vine-ripened tomatoes

420 g can of mixed beans (kidney, cannellini)

2 green onions, finely chopped

1 tablespoon olive oil

Packet of baby spinach leaves

1 tablespoon lemon juice

1 large red capsicum, finely chopped

1 roasted beetroot, sliced

4 pieces of Atlantic salmon

Combine all ingredients except for fish and serve with 4 pieces of grilled salmon.

Serves 4

KING PRAWN AND MANGO SALAD

300 g natural reduced-fat yoghurt

1 tablespoon chopped coriander

1 teaspoon fish sauce

1 teaspoon brown sugar

Finely grated rind of 1 lime

⅓ baby cos lettuce, washed and sliced

½ continental cucumber, sliced with a peeler

1 mango, peeled and sliced

100 g snow peas, blanched

12 cooked king prawns, peeled and deveined

1 Combine yoghurt, coriander, fish sauce, sugar and lime rind. Refrigerate until required.

2 Divide remaining ingredients between serving plates and drizzle with yoghurt dressing.

Serves 2

BAKED FISH

2 teaspoons honey

1 teaspoon peanut oil

1 small, hot chilli, finely sliced

1 teaspoon grated ginger

1 teaspoon lemon juice

1 tablespoon salt-reduced soy sauce

2 green onions, finely chopped

1 kg white fish

1 Preheat oven to 200°C.

2 Place all ingredients except green onions and fish into a screw-top jar and shake well.

3 Brush fish with marinade and bake for 20 minutes on a greased oven tray.

4 Sprinkle fish with onions and serve with salad.

Serves 4

VEGETABLE FRITTATA

½ cup oats

1 tablespoon canola or olive oil

1 onion, grated

1 carrot, coarsely grated

100 g cooked broccoli

150 g cooked pumpkin

5 eggs

⅔ cup low-fat milk

1 medium tomato, sliced

1 cup 50% reduced-fat tasty cheese

1 Toast oats under grill until brown.

2 Heat oil in pan; sauté onion and carrot until onion is tender.

3 Remove pan from heat; add broccoli and pumpkin, and top with oats.

4 Beat eggs with milk; pour over vegetables in pan. Cook over gentle heat until eggs are set.

5 Top with tomato and cheese, and grill until cheese has melted.

6 Serve with a large green salad for a delicious, light meal.

Serves 8

LAMB WITH BARBECUED VEGETABLES

4 cloves garlic, chopped

¼ cup rosemary, chopped

2 tablespoons olive oil

500 g lamb tenderloins

2 zucchinis, sliced

1 red capsicum, deseeded and sliced

2 finger eggplants, sliced

1   In a bowl, mix the garlic, rosemary and olive oil. Place half the mixture in a separate bowl, add the lamb and set aside.

2   In a second bowl, place the vegetables with the rest of the garlic and rosemary mixture and season well with salt and pepper. Stir to coat well.

3   Cook the vegetables on a hot barbecue or under the grill for 3 minutes each side, and set aside in a warm place covered with aluminium foil.

4   Season the lamb with salt and pepper and cook on the barbecue or under the grill for 3 minutes each side, or to your liking. Let the lamb rest for 5 minutes while you serve out the vegetables, and then top the vegetables with the lamb.

Serves 4

GRILLED PRAWNS AND VEGETABLE SALAD

6–8 green prawns, cleaned and deveined

2 tablespoons pesto

1 teaspoon olive oil

1 corn cob

1 red capsicum, diced

1 green capsicum, diced

1 small zucchini, diced

½ punnet cherry tomatoes

1 Mix prawns with pesto and set aside.

2 Heat oil in a pan; add corn, capsicum and zucchini and sauté until lightly browned. Add tomatoes and cook until skins blister.

3 Add prawns and heat through. Serve with vegetable salad.

Serves 1

CHILLI AND LIME CHICKEN SALAD

1 cup water

1 cup salt-reduced chicken stock

500 g chicken breast fillets

1 large carrot

1 large red capsicum, sliced thinly

½ Chinese cabbage, shredded finely

2 green onions, finely chopped

1 cup bean sprouts

½ cup firmly packed fresh coriander leaves

¼ cup lime juice

2 tablespoons sweet chilli sauce

1 clove garlic, crushed

1 tablespoon oyster sauce

1 teaspoon sesame oil

1 Place water and stock in a large saucepan and bring to the boil.

2 Reduce heat; add chicken and simmer for about 10 minutes or until chicken is cooked through. Allow chicken to cool in cooking liquid before draining.

3 Discard liquid; slice chicken into thin slices.

4 Meanwhile, halve the carrot crosswise and cut each half lengthwise into 2 mm wide strips; then cut the lengths into matchsticks.

5 Place chicken and carrot in a large bowl with the capsicum, cabbage, onion, sprouts and coriander.

6 Add lime juice, chilli sauce, garlic, oyster sauce and sesame oil, and toss to combine.

Serves 4

Tips and tricks for your 4 week program

- Avoid starting your new program with an intense 'all or nothing' approach and then falling off the rails. Start small and build each week.

- The earlier you eat breakfast, the better it will be for your metabolism.

- Remember that you need some carbs at both breakfast and lunch to maximise metabolism.

- The importance of eating a protein-rich breakfast early and aiming for a small dinner by 7 pm cannot be overemphasised.

- Never leave the house without a protein-rich snack with you.

- Snack on vegetable soup or cut-up vegetables when you find yourself hungry.

- Keep your weekends low-key so that you can concentrate on your program.

- If for some reason you end up eating more than you should, compensate with extra training or a light meal the next day.

- Use light sauces and dressings to flavour your salads and vegetables.

- Measure all liquid cooking oil that you use.

- Monitor your calories using on online program such as CalorieKing.

- Aim to drink 2–3 cups of green tea a day.

- Take a 4 week break from alcohol.

- Weigh and measure your body each week, at the same time of day.

4 week weight loss snack list

150 g natural yoghurt with ½ cup berries

4 wholegrain crackers with 2 slices (40 g) reduced-fat cheese

1 piece of fruit and 15 nuts

1 carrot with small container of hommus

Small skim coffee with 15 nuts

30 g trail mix

1 low-fat ice-cream on a stick and 1 piece of fruit

2 rye crackers with 2 tablespoons of cottage cheese

20 g dark chocolate with a small skim milk coffee

1 sushi roll with a vegetable juice

4 week weight loss checklist

1. Get breakfast right – and eat it before 8 am.

2. Get your snack balance right.

3. Get your lunch balance right.

4. Have soup once a day.

5. Have a protein-rich afternoon snack.

6. Eat dinner by 7 pm.

7. Train and walk.

8. Eat some nuts every day.

9. Drink mainly water or green/herbal tea.

10. Have a meal off occasionally.

When you have 3 months

❧ *The scary thing is that it is really not that difficult to gain 10 kilos – a couple of hundred extra calories a day, over a 12 month period, and bang, there it is.*

People are often surprised to learn that **even if we maintain the same eating and exercise habits over the course of a year,** in our current environment, in which so many of us lead relatively sedentary lives, we are still likely to be gaining small amounts of weight. The reason for this is that once we reach adulthood, unless we are exceptionally vigilant and constantly adjust our food intake and the type and quantity of training we do, our metabolic rate gets slower. If you then also consider that many of us naturally move less as we get older, again resulting in fewer calories being burnt, it becomes clear why so many people develop weight issues throughout their adult lives.

Scientific research has confirmed that people are more likely to keep on track with any diet or exercise program if they lose weight initially. So if your ultimate goal is to lose 5–10 kilos, it's a good idea to kick-start your program with a week or two of a relatively strict food and exercise 'strip' plan. Such a regime will give your body a quick jolt, allowing you to drop a couple of kilos over a week or two, and this is often the psychological boost we need to keep focused and on track for a longer period. Once you have kick-started your program, you will be ready to make some more gradual changes to both your calorie intake and your training program that will see you continue to shift a kilo or so each week and move towards a 5–10 kilo loss over a 3 month period.

The difference between shorter-term weight loss programs and a 3 month or 6 month approach is that once you need to lose 10 kilos or more, you are looking at making significant lifestyle changes. For whatever reason, you have developed some bad habits. You need to identify them and gradually replace them with habits that are conducive to weight control in the long term. Give some thought to this, and try to pinpoint the various habits that collectively may have caused you to gain weight over months if not years. Then think about what specific, practical actions you could take to shift them.

Common habits that contribute to weight gain

HABIT	SUGGESTED CHANGE
Drinking milk coffee at work.	Drink herbal tea.
Drinking large cups of coffee.	Switch to small.
Overeating at night.	Have a protein-rich mid-afternoon snack.
Picking up snacks on the run.	Always carry a protein-rich snack with you.
Eating after dinner.	Snack on low-calorie foods only.
Drinking alcohol every day.	Drink alcohol only on weekends.
Skipping breakfast.	Grab a breakfast shake on the go.
Adding sugar to coffee.	Wean yourself off added sugar.
Eating dinner late at night.	Have your main meal at lunchtime.
Training inefficiently.	Get a personal trainer once a week.

Once you have identified your high-risk food or exercise habits, you need to allow time to change them, and the only way to do this is to practise. This means constantly reminding yourself of the new habits you need to adopt and each and every day striving to make these changes. For example, if you know that you need to get into the habit of eating breakfast every day, you might put a note reminding you to do this in a prominent spot in your kitchen, or you might set the alarm on your mobile phone to remind you to grab something before you leave home. Once you have made it through the first couple of weeks of actively working towards developing a new habit, you will be well on your way to cementing the habit in the long term. Research suggests it takes up to 12 weeks to deeply entrench any new habit.

The next thing you need to do is ditch the 'all or nothing' approach to dieting once. At times we will all consume more calories than we need or skip training sessions, but it is not these one-off occurrences that impact on your ability to lose weight. So, if you have a one-off treat, or a few too many glasses of wine once in a while, or miss the odd training session, this doesn't mean that you've blown it completely. The important thing is to get back on track at the next meal or training session. Clearly, though, if you use occasional lapses as an excuse to fall back into bad habits, such as skipping breakfast, not eating enough vegetables and having a high-carb dinner at night, you cannot expect to lose weight.

Unlike more rapid weight loss programs, in which calorie intake needs to be tightly controlled, when you have a longer time frame in which to lose weight you can be a little more flexible while still losing half a kilo to a kilo each week. **The key to losing weight over this longer period is to have a few key eating habits firmly in place and then to learn how and when to change certain aspects of your diet and/or your training to ensure that you continue to lose weight over the 6–12 weeks.** For example, while restricting your calories to a certain level may help you lose 3–5 kilos over 3–4 weeks, it is unlikely that this same number of calories will work for you throughout a 12 week period. In most cases it is necessary to keep changing your calorie intake so that the body's cells are challenged and continue to burn body fat effectively.

10 key strategies for your 3 month weight loss program

1. EAT A 300 CALORIE BREAKFAST

It is going to be very hard to get on top of your weight issues in the long term if you are not prepared to commit to eating breakfast every single day and to aim to have it eaten by 8 am. While on a short-term weight loss plan you may limit your breakfast to 200 calories, on average we need a 300–400 calorie breakfast to optimise our metabolic rate. The other breakfast weight loss trick is to make sure that your breakfast contains 15–20 grams of protein. High-carbohydrate breakfasts, including cereal, plain toast, and yoghurt and fruit, may seem 'healthy', but they contain a much higher proportion of carbohydrate than protein, which leaves you vulnerable to hunger and high insulin levels throughout the day. Bumping up the protein content of your breakfast is a great way to kick-start your metabolism and your weight loss.

300 calorie breakfasts

1 slice wholegrain bread + 1 egg + 130 g can baked beans

⅓ cup oats + 1 cup milk + 1 small skim coffee

1 slice wholegrain toast + 1 slice light cheese + 25 g low-fat ham

200 g natural yoghurt + 2 teaspoons oats + 1 cup berries

1 Brekkie Shake (see recipe on page 100)

1 meal replacement shake + 1 slice toast with light cream cheese

Brekkie Scramble (see recipe on page 99)

1 Breakfast Wrap (see recipe below on page 99)

¾ cup bran cereal + 1 cup milk + 1 small skim coffee

Large skim coffee + 1 small bowl fruit salad

BREAKFAST RECIPES

BREAKFAST WRAP

1 egg

Canola oil spray

1 slice 97% fat-free bacon

1 slice tomato

1 lettuce leaf

1 piece wholemeal/
wholegrain wrap bread

2 teaspoons low-fat
mayonnaise

1 Poach egg, or fry using canola oil spray.

2 Lightly sear bacon.

3 Place egg, bacon, tomato and lettuce on bread, drizzle with mayonnaise, wrap and serve.

Serves 1

BREKKIE SCRAMBLE

Canola oil spray

½ brown onion, finely
chopped

1 tomato, diced

30 g mushrooms, sliced

2 free-range eggs, lightly
beaten

30 g grated reduced-fat tasty
cheese

25 g 97% fat-free ham, diced

1 Heat a non-stick pan over medium heat. Lightly spray pan with oil. Add the onion, tomato and mushrooms and cook for about 1 minute or until translucent. Add eggs and allow to set.

2 Once the eggs are almost set but still slightly soft, add cheese and ham and mix together to make a scramble.

Serves 1

BREKKIE SHAKE

200 ml low-fat milk	Blend all ingredients until smooth.
100 ml vanilla yoghurt	
½ cup berries	
1 teaspoon vanilla protein powder	
1 teaspoon honey	**Serves 1**

2. KEEP YOUR DINNER SMALL

The average dinner clocks in at 500 calories or more, and that is without any chocolate, alcohol or dessert. Many of us eat lightly during the day and arrive home starving late at night, and then overeat. Since we are likely to spend the remaining hours before bedtime sitting or lying down, this is not a time when we need a lot of calories, especially from carbohydrates.

So commit to keeping your dinner light, especially during the week. **Light means just 400 calories** – a soup, a small portion of meat, and lots of salad and vegetables. Avoid large portions of rice or pasta. Keeping your dinner light will help you burn extra calories overnight, give you the freedom to eat a little more at weekends, and mean that you are more likely to wake up hungry for a substantial, protein-rich breakfast.

400 calorie dinners

150 g white fish + roasted pumpkin, eggplant, zucchini
100 g lean steak + 1 small jacket potato + salad
100 g Atlantic salmon + stir-fried carrots, bok choy and broccoli
150 g grilled chicken breast + ½ corn cob + salad
1 mountain bread pizza topped with 100 g chicken breast + vegetables
3 lean lamb cutlets with ½ cup mashed potato + vegetables
¾ cup cooked pasta + 100 g lean mince + vegetables
Stir-fried prawns + ½ cup cooked rice + vegetables
2 pork chops + ½ cup roasted sweet potato + salad
1 small piece of lasagne + salad

3. CUT OUT THE EXTRAS

It doesn't matter if it's a coffee, the extra sauce or dressing you add to your food, or the beer or two at night, **extra calories count, and for many of us this means the difference between losing weight or not**. The most common extras that have snuck into our diets over the years include the liquid calories found in milk-based coffees; flavoured juices, waters and energy drinks; and sauces, spreads and dressings.

If you have noticed your weight creeping up, paying attention for a day or two to how many little extras creep into your diet each day will give you some insight into why this has happened. If we simply ate three meals and a couple of small snacks a day, few of us would have weight issues, but many of us are putting food in our mouth 20 or more times a day. This not only disrupts our hormones and digestive balance, but it also means we are consuming too many calories. Cut back and you will lose weight.

EXTRAS CHECKLIST	CALORIES
1 teaspoon sugar	15
1 tablespoon olive oil	160
1 tablespoon tomato sauce	25
1 small latte	100
1 row of block chocolate	100
1 chocolate biscuit	100
1 tablespoon mayonnaise	60
1 teaspoon honey/jam	15

4. LIMIT ALCOHOL

Alcohol, like chocolate, is a highly charged issue for many people. Some weight loss clients say they would do anything rather than skip their nightly glass of wine while preparing dinner. There is nothing wrong with enjoying a glass or two of wine, but often a glass can quickly turn into half a bottle with an extra 500 calories to match.

The interesting thing about regular wine drinkers is that when you really examine their behaviour, often they are not drinking for pleasure or enjoyment or even taste, but rather out of habit. Similar to eating chocolate after dinner, it can become way too easy to grab the bottle of wine and pour yourself a glass the second you walk in the door, and then spend the rest of the night slowly finishing the bottle.

With a gradual, sustainable weight loss program, we have 100–200 extra calories a day to play with, and if you love your wine you can use some of your calories to enjoy a small glass or two each day. Another option is to drink only on weekends, ideally enjoying no more than 2–3 glasses. From a weight loss point of view, it is much better to enjoy your alcohol on one or two occasions rather than in smaller amounts spread over the course of a week. The reason for this is twofold. First, once you start to drink, it is likely that you will drink more than you intended to. Second, drinking a small amount each day will mean that you are less likely to be burning the calories you have consumed via your food, and the fewer times this happens when you are trying to lose weight, the better.

Calories in various alcoholic drinks

	CALORIES
Small glass of wine (120 ml)	90
Small glass of champagne (120 ml)	85
Small glass of low-alcohol wine (120 ml)	80
Large glass of wine (240 ml)	150
Bottle of wine (700 ml)	700
2 regular beers (750 ml)	300
Low-carbohydrate beer (355 ml)	120
Pre-mixed spirit (375 ml)	160
Bourbon and cola	125
Bourbon and diet cola	70
Vodka and orange	160
Vodka, lime and soda	60

5. EAT PLENTY OF SALAD AND VEGETABLES

You need at least 2 cups of low-calorie salad, vegetables or soup to bulk up both lunch and dinner, as well as some cut-up vegetables to snack on during the day. The only way to achieve this is to plan ahead and stock the fridge with what you need. Many of us are getting nowhere near this amount.

The benefits of eating more vegetables are numerous for both general health and for weight loss. From a weight loss perspective, vegetables are exceptionally low in calories and are also the ideal food to provide you with the bulk you need to avoid feeling as if you are starving. Feeling full and satiated is one of the key aspects of a successful weight loss regime.

The following tips will help ensure you get the quantity of vegetables and salad you need each and every day to feel satisfied while you are steadily losing weight.

- Cook up a batch of vegetable soup each week (see recipe on page 76).

- Prepare your salad for the week ahead on Sunday night or afternoon. (You can always add the dressing or avocado or cheese later.)

- Never leave the house without two kinds of vegetables to snack on.

- When you walk in the door at night, get into the habit of grabbing a vegetable snack rather than crackers or nuts.

- Always make sure your dinner plate is half filled with vegetables or salad.

Here are some ideas for easy, tasty vegetable snacks.

VEGETABLE SNACK	SERVE WITH
Cucumber strips	Low-fat tzatziki
Carrot	Low-fat hummus
Red capsicum	Extra-light cream cheese
Celery	2 teaspoons peanut butter
Snow peas	Tomato salsa
Broccoli and cauliflower florets	Cheese sauce

These vegetable fritters also make a great snack.

THREE-VEGETABLE FRITTERS

1 cup white self-raising flour

½ cup wholemeal self-raising flour

½ teaspoon salt

1 medium carrot, grated

1 medium zucchini, grated

½ cup reduced-fat grated cheese

3 eggs, lightly beaten

1 cup milk

1 tablespoon olive oil

1 Sift flours and salt into a large bowl. Add vegetables and cheese.

2 Combine eggs and milk. Stir liquid ingredients into dry ingredients.

3 Heat oil in a large non-stick pan and spoon the mixture into the pan in 4 roughly equal amounts; cook the fritters until lightly browned.

Serves 4

6. LEARN TO COMPENSATE

It is not necessary to be a diet purist to successfully lose weight, but a crucial skill of those who both successfully lose weight and also manage to keep it off is that they are able to self-regulate their food intake. This means that when they do have a heavy meal, a big weekend or one too many treats, they know how to hold back a little for a meal or a few days afterwards to balance out the extra calories. Similarly, they also know that at times they may need to do a little more training to compensate when they have skipped training sessions or eaten a little too much.

The important thing is to recognise when this is starting to become a pattern and to develop a contingency plan to manage it. For example, if you know you will be eating out, make it a rule that you will eat lightly the next day to compensate. Or train for an extra 30 minutes at the gym the following day to burn the extra calories.

If we always keep mindful of working towards a balance of 'calories in equal calories out', it becomes easy to make a habit of compensating. If you are aiming to lose around 10 kilos over a 3 month period, obviously you are not going to be able to eat a chocolate bar or a piece of cake every single day and then spend an intense hour at the gym working it off. If, however, you have a special occasion coming up, such as a birthday, a work lunch or a conference, you can plan ahead and eat more lightly at another meal to compensate. Or if you decide to be a bit more relaxed about your food and exercise regime on the weekends, then you may have to be stricter during the week.

Each person needs to find a balance between lifestyle and weight loss that works for them, but compensating will work for everyone. Here are some common food scenarios you may find challenging when it comes to controlling your calorie intake and some ideas on ways to compensate:

CHALLENGING SCENARIO	WAY TO COMPENSATE
Restaurant meal	Salad or soup for the meal before
Dessert	Walk to and from dinner
4–5 alcoholic drinks	1 hour extra cardio training
Work lunch	Soup for dinner
Big weekend	Week of light dinners
Work conference	Salad for lunch each day
Block of chocolate	1 hour of extra training
1 glass of wine	No carbs at night

7. UNDERSTAND THE IMPORTANCE OF CARDIO TRAINING

Most of us know that cardio training, the type of exercise that significantly increases your heart rate – whether it is running, gym classes or fast walking – plays an important part in weight loss and also in long-term weight maintenance. But not everyone is aware that the secret of success when it comes to cardio training is to strike the right balance between effective calorie burning, hunger management and weight loss. Too much training and you may find yourself very hungry and more likely to eat more to compensate. Too little, and you may not continually lose weight.

Another thing to consider is that when people try to increase the amount of cardio training they are doing, they have the belief that they need to train for at least an hour in order to get results. Commonly this sees individuals sit on a bike at the gym or walk on a treadmill mindlessly simply so they can tick the box that they have completed their cardio. Often they don't enjoy the training, they give themselves permission to eat more calories because they have trained and 'deserve it', and then over weeks they become bored and tired and end up hating doing cardio workouts completely.

To avoid this, and considering that any type of cardio training is great for our health and also for weight loss, it is a misconception that successful weight loss will require you to train for at least an hour a day. This is not so. We now know that a much better approach is to go for quality over quantity. That is, commit to short bursts of 10–20 minutes of high-intensity activity that get your heart rate up, burn 200–300 calories in a 20–30 minute session at least every other day, and also aim to move a lot during your day. This more controlled amount of cardio has several benefits. Most people can handle 20–30 minutes of cardio without finding it mind-numbingly boring; it is unlikely to make you excessively hungry; and best of all you will still be burning a sufficient number of extra calories to help you lose weight.

For the first 4–6 weeks of your 3 month program, this approach, in combination with your 3 month eating plan, is likely to see you dropping between half a kilo and 2 kilos each week. But as you get fitter and your body gets used to surviving on fewer calories, you will need to change your training program regularly to keep challenging your body and losing weight. For example, if you are training 3 days a week, you may need to go to 5 days, or vice versa. If you are training for 30 minutes, you may need to do 60 minutes, or if you train in the morning, you may need to switch to evenings.

❧ *If you return from any of your training sessions feeling like you could do it all over again, it means you are not training hard enough – it is time to up the ante.*

Ways you can change your cardio program

1. Change the treadmill settings to walk or run on an incline, or interval train.
2. Turn up the resistance level on the gym machine by at least 2 levels.
3. Do cardio after weights.
4. Add 10 minutes of cardio to any gym class you go to.
5. Walk or run to the gym.
6. Jog for one minute before walking for 3–5 minutes.
7. Find hills or steps to climb on walks.
8. Alternate machines every 10 minutes.
9. Add 10 minutes of skipping into your day.
10. Add an extra 5 minutes to each machine you train with.

8. KEEP AS ACTIVE AS POSSIBLE

If, like so many people today, you spend much of your day sitting down, an exercise session once a day may not be enough to support weight loss. In fact, sitting down all day can do far more damage to our metabolism – that is, the body's ability to burn calories – than any other lifestyle factor. To manage this modern-day dilemma we need to proactively add more movement into our day and accept that this is something we will need to do every day for the rest of our lives. Unfortunately, for many people an exercise session once a day just does not cut it. We also need to walk and move as much as we can to undo all the damage that has occurred from sitting down for most of the day.

For the average person this will mean aiming for a 20–30 minute walk each day in addition to your cardio training. This may mean getting out at lunchtime to walk, getting off the bus or train a stop earlier and walking the rest of the way, or going for a daily pre-breakfast or post-dinner walk. If you respond well to numbers, invest in a pedometer and start tracking your steps, aiming for a minimum of 10,000 a day.

9. MONITOR YOUR HUNGER

As the period of time in which you wish to lose weight increases from a few weeks to a few months, so too does the need to monitor the way your appetite responds to the changes in your food habits, and you need to adjust your calorie intake accordingly. For example, when you start your program on a certain number of calories, it is likely that this number of calories will sustain you for a few weeks before you start to get hungrier and feel that you need more food.

Hunger is a strong physiological sign that your body has burnt the food from your last meal and that you need to eat again. Ideally, your meals and snacks will keep you full and satisfied for at least 3 hours, so if after a few weeks you notice that you are frequently feeling hungrier, this is a strong sign that you may need to increase the size of your meals.

Generally speaking, if you experience true hunger (as opposed to a desire to eat because you see a chocolate biscuit) less than 2 hours after your meal or snack, this is a sign that you need to eat a little more. This may occur, for example, if you have cut your carbohydrate intake back too severely, or if you have not included enough salad or vegetables to bulk up your meals. Many people experience extreme hunger and sugar cravings in the late afternoon because they don't get the balance right at lunchtime. If you are ravenous at 10 am, two hours after breakfast, this means your breakfast needs to be a little larger, while hunger after dinner may suggest that you have cut the carbs back a little too much.

Adjusting your food intake

HUNGER	WHAT TO CHANGE
Early morning	Add ½ cup carbs to your dinner.
Mid-morning	Add 100 calories to your breakfast.
11 am	Increase the size of your breakfast.
2 pm	Increase the carb portion of your lunch.
5 pm	Add a protein shake to your mid-afternoon snack.
After dinner	Add ½ cup carbs to your dinner.

10. ADJUST YOUR CARBS

When you have committed to a reduced-carbohydrate style of eating and are losing weight, it can be hard to understand why you would need to eat more carbs to enhance weight loss. The reality is that after you have been following a reduced-carb style of eating and also training regularly for a period of time, at some point you will need to eat more carbohydrate in order to fuel the muscle to continue to burn fat as efficiently as it can. The first sign that you may need to do this is if you start to crave carbs, sugar in particular. This means that your muscles are crying out for extra fuel and that you may have not been having enough carbs with your breakfast or lunch. Similarly, if you are craving sugar all the time, it is a sign that you simply need a little more food. If this is the case, add one extra serve of carbs to your breakfast and lunch and see if this helps. If you are still hungry, you may need to add extra to your snacks and even dinner as well, until you are having 1–2 serves of carbs every time you eat. Once you are eating carbs at every meal, you also have the option of dropping them at dinner again for a period of time if your weight loss slows.

Serves of carbs

1 serve = 15 g total carbohydrate

1 slice of wholegrain bread

2 wholegrain crackers

4 rye crackers

1 piece of fruit

100 g yoghurt

⅓ cup cereal

1 small potato/piece of sweet potato

½ cup corn

½ cup beans

1 small wrap bread

Sample 3 month food plan

This menu contains an average of 1500–1600 calories per day.

	MONDAY	TUESDAY	WEDNESDAY
BREAKFAST	2 poached eggs + 1 slice wholegrain toast	2 slices wholegrain toast + 130 g can baked beans	¾ cup bran cereal + ½ cup berries
MID-MORNING	100 g natural yoghurt + ½ cup berries	2 rye crackers + 40 g reduced-fat cheese	Small skim coffee + 1 piece of fruit
LUNCH	95 g can tuna/salmon + 130 g can mixed beans + ½ cup corn + mixed salad + 1 tsp olive oil dressing	100 g grilled chicken breast + 2 pieces flatbread + mixed salad + 1 tsp olive oil dressing	¾ cup brown rice + 95 g can tuna mixed with red capsicum and 1 tsp sweet chilli sauce
MID-AFTERNOON	10 walnuts + 1 piece of fruit	1 nut-based snack bar	2 corn thins + thin spread peanut butter + 1 apple
DINNER	150 g grilled fish + 1 piece sweet potato + vegetables stir-fried in 1 tsp olive oil	100 g lean steak fillet + 1 small baked potato + salad	100 g grilled chicken + 1 baked potato + salad

THURSDAY	FRIDAY	SATURDAY	SUNDAY
⅓ cup oats + 1 cup low-fat milk + 2 kiwi fruit or ½ cup mixed berries	2 poached eggs + 1 slice wholegrain toast	⅓ cup oats + 1 cup low-fat milk + 2 kiwi fruit or ½ cup mixed berries	Bacon and egg wrap
Pack of chick nuts + 1 piece of fruit	Small skim coffee + 1 cup berries	1 piece of fruit	1 piece of fruit
95 g can tuna/ salmon + 130 g can mixed beans + 1 piece flatbread + mixed salad + 1 tsp olive oil dressing	100 g grilled chicken breast + 2 pieces flatbread + mixed salad	Jacket potato topped with red salmon + ⅓ cup cottage cheese + 1 chopped tomato + 1 piece of fruit	Chicken caesar salad
2 rye crackers with reduced-fat cream cheese + 1 tomato + 10 walnuts	2 corn thins + thin spread avocado + 1 apple	15 almonds + 1 piece of fruit	10 walnuts
100 g piece grilled lamb + 100 g baked sweet potato + vegetables stir-fried in 1 tsp olive oil	100 g chicken breast + ½ cup brown rice + stir-fried vegetables in oyster sauce	150 g tuna steak on sweet potato mash + Asian greens	Vegetable soup + 100 g grilled Atlantic salmon

RECIPES FOR YOUR 3 MONTH PLAN

The recipes featured here contain between 350 and 400 calories and are good dinner options for your 3 month plan.

CHICKEN WALDORF SALAD

½ cup pecans

¼ cup whole-egg mayonnaise

1 tablespoon extra-virgin olive oil

1 tablespoon white wine vinegar

1 tablespoon finely chopped fresh chives

1 teaspoon honey

500 g grilled chicken breast

1 small avocado, thinly sliced

2 green apples, cored, halved, finely chopped

2 celery sticks, trimmed, finely chopped

1 packet baby rocket leaves

1 Preheat oven to 180°C. Spread the pecans over a baking tray and heat in oven for 5 minutes or until golden brown and fragrant. Remove from oven and set aside for 5 minutes to cool.

2 Meanwhile, to make the dressing, whisk together the mayonnaise, oil, vinegar, chives and honey in a small bowl.

3 Place the chicken, avocado, apple, celery, rocket and pecans in a large bowl and toss gently to combine.

4 Spoon the salad onto a platter. Drizzle with oil dressing to serve.

Serves 4

STUFFED ZUCCHINIS

2 large zucchinis

¼ cup raw brown rice

Olive oil

1 small onion, chopped

¼ cup chopped capsicum

1 small carrot, grated

6 small mushrooms, sliced

1 small tomato, chopped

1 tablespoon parsley

¼ cup reduced-fat grated cheese

1 Place zucchinis in water and cook for 3 minutes. Drain and cool under running water.

2 Cook rice until tender. Halve the zucchinis and scoop out flesh (keep shells). Chop flesh finely.

3 Heat oil in pan and fry onion until soft. Add zucchini, capsicum, carrot and mushrooms and cook until tender.

4 Add tomato and parsley and fold into the rice. Spoon the zucchini mixture into the zucchini shells and top with grated cheese. Bake in the oven at 180°C for 20 minutes until lightly browned.

Serves 2

GRILLED PRAWNS AND VEGETABLE SALAD

6–8 green prawns, cleaned and deveined

2 tablespoons pesto

1 teaspoon olive oil

½ cup fresh or canned corn

1 red capsicum, diced

1 green capsicum, diced

1 small zucchini, diced

½ punnet cherry tomatoes

1 Mix prawns with pesto and set aside.

2 Heat oil in pan; add corn, capsicum and zucchini and sauté until lightly browned. Add tomatoes and cook until skins blister.

3 Add prawns, heat through and serve with the vegetable salad.

Serves 1

ROASTED VEGETABLE SALAD WITH MOZZARELLA

2 slices mozzarella cheese (50 mm slices)

2 small slices sourdough bread

Light caesar dressing

1 eggplant, finely sliced, grilled

1 red capsicum, chopped into coarse chunks

Grilled asparagus spears, chopped

Mixed lettuce leaves

4 Roma tomatoes, coarsely chopped

1　Place cheese on bread and grill until cheese is soft.

2　Add dressing to mixed salad ingredients and serve with cheese toasts.

Serves 4 as a side dish

ROAST PUMPKIN AND BEAN SALAD

600 g pumpkin, cut into large pieces

1 red onion, cut into wedges

1 tablespoon olive oil

½ teaspoon cracked pepper

¼ teaspoon dried oregano

420 g can four bean mix, drained

3 lean bacon rashers, cut into strips and pan-fried

Dressing

2 teaspoons seeded mustard

1 tablespoon balsamic vinegar

3 tablespoons olive oil

¼ teaspoon sugar

1 Place pumpkin and onion in a freezer bag, add oil, pepper and oregano, and shake bag until vegetables are evenly coated.

2 Tip pumpkin and onion onto a baking tray and cook in a preheated oven at 200ºC for 25–30 minutes.

3 In a large serving bowl, combine roasted vegetables and drained four bean mix. Combine dressing ingredients, pour over the vegetable mixture and garnish with bacon.

Serves 4 as a side dish

LAMB CUTLETS WITH BEAN AND SPINACH SALAD

8 frenched lamb cutlets

Balsamic vinegar

1 tablespoon olive oil

1 Spanish onion, sliced

420 g can cannellini beans

Baby spinach leaves

2 Roma tomatoes, sliced

1 Preheat oven to 200°C. Place lamb cutlets in an oven dish, drizzle with balsamic vinegar and bake for 15–20 minutes.

2 While the lamb is heating, heat oil in a pan over medium heat and fry onion until soft. Add beans and cook until soft.

3 Transfer the mixture to a bowl and add spinach leaves and tomato, mixing lightly to combine.

4 Serve lamb cutlets on a bed of bean and spinach salad.

Serves 4

SESAME CHICKEN STIR-FRY

1 tablespoon sunflower oil

500 g chicken breast, cut into strips

2 teaspoons salt-reduced soy sauce

2 teaspoons honey

1 clove garlic, finely chopped

1 red capsicum, sliced

1 cup snow peas

1 large carrot, sliced

1 large zucchini, sliced

1 cup broccoli florets

2 cups cooked brown rice

2 tablespoons sesame seeds

1 Heat oil in a pan; add chicken and cook until browned.

2 Add soy sauce, honey and garlic and cook for a further 5 minutes.

3 Add vegetables and brown rice and cook for a further 10 minutes.

4 Serve topped with sesame seeds.

Serves 4

CHICKEN WITH PUMPKIN AND SPINACH

500 g butternut pumpkin, cubed

1 tablespoon olive oil

1 red onion, diced

2 cloves garlic, finely chopped

1 bunch English spinach

2 teaspoons water

500 g chicken breast, diced and cooked

1 lemon

1 Boil, steam or microwave cubed pumpkin until soft.

2 Heat oil in a pan over medium heat. Add onion and garlic and cook until soft.

3 Add pumpkin and cook until browned.

4 Chop sufficient spinach to make 2 cups; place in a bowl with 2 teaspoons of water and set aside.

5 Add cooked chicken and the spinach and water mixture; cook until spinach wilts. Once heated through, serve with a squeeze of lemon.

Serves 4

GRILLED PORK CHOPS

1½ cups panko (Japanese breadcrumbs)

4 lean pork loin chops

2 tablespoons Dijon mustard

500 g roasted pumpkin, cubed and heated through

4 cups mixed, cooked green vegetables (such as broccoli, green beans and zucchini)

1 Preheat oven to 200ºC. Spread panko over baking sheet and bake for 5–10 minutes until golden brown.

2 Coat chops with mustard and dip in panko. Bake in the oven until golden brown.

3 Serve pork chops with roast pumpkin and green vegetables.

Serves 4

LAMB HALOUMI SALAD

200 g lean, grilled lamb backstrap

Mixed rocket and spinach leaves

20 walnuts

Reduced-fat haloumi cheese

100 g semi-dried tomatoes

100 g or 1 bunch of grilled asparagus

Caramelised balsamic vinegar

Flesh of 1 sliced mango

Mix ingredients together to make a simple salad.

Serves 2

Tips and tricks for your 3 month program

- Over a 3 month period there will inevitably be times when you go a little off track, whether it is over a weekend, a week or even a few weeks. The most important thing is to get back on track as soon as you can.

- Accept that over this period of time there will be times when you lose weight and times when you don't. This is part of the process of losing weight.

- To maximise weight loss, the best time to keep your carb intake low is at night.

- If your weight has been stable for 3 weeks or more, it is time to make some changes to your calories and/or your training.

- Try having green tea after meals to boost your metabolism. Other proven metabolism lifters include eating a protein-rich breakfast, such as eggs on wholegrain bread, early in the morning; drinking 600 ml of ice-cold water after meals; adding hot chilli to sauces and soups; and exercising before breakfast.

- Make a list of 10 quick and easy meals and 10 nutritionally balanced snack foods and stick them on your fridge as inspiration for times when you arrive home late and tired and can't think what you feel like eating.

- Nothing is more important during a period of weight loss than training regularly. You need to train at least 3 times a week to get results.

- When you eat out, distinguish between special occasions and your regular weekly outings – let loose on special occasions but try to stay on track for your regular meals out.

- If you find yourself about to overindulge, create a distraction – go for a walk, call a friend or take a shower. Often a diversion is all you need to remind you of your dietary goals and keep your food and nutrition on track.

- It is better to have a few drinks on one night each week than 1 or 2 drinks each day.

3 month weight loss snack list

100 g yoghurt + 1 piece of fruit

4 wholegrain crackers with 2 slices of light cheese

Nut-based snack bar

Small hummus + cut-up vegetables

Small skim coffee + 1 piece of fruit

30 g trail mix + small skim coffee

150 g yoghurt + ½ cup berries

2 rye crackers with 2 teaspoons peanut butter

20 g dark chocolate + 1 piece of fruit

Small skim coffee +1 piece of biscotti

3 month weight loss checklist

1. Eat a 300 calorie breakfast.
2. Keep your dinner small.
3. Cut out the extras.
4. Limit alcohol.
5. Eat plenty of salad and vegetables.
6. Learn to compensate.
7. Understand the importance of cardio training.
8. Keep as active as possible.
9. Monitor your hunger.
10. Adjust your carbs.

When it's all going too slowly

❀ *'It's really difficult to stay motivated when I am working so hard and seeing no results.'*

You started your weight loss plan with all guns blazing. You have got organised and planned all of your meals. You have exercised almost every day for the past 6 or 8 weeks and lost 3–5 kilos relatively easily. Then all of a sudden the weight loss stopped. You had a week in which you barely lost anything and you vowed to try even harder, but when you didn't lose anything the following week you felt so frustrated that you threw in the towel and stopped the program altogether.

There are a few reasons why weight loss tends to slow 6–8 weeks into a program. Sometimes the body has simply become used to the reduced number of calories, or after a few weeks the type of training you are doing has become ineffectual and needs to be changed. More often, though, it comes down to our attitude towards weight loss and our expectations, and also the way we react when things become a little more challenging.

For starters, we tend to go wrong by expecting weight loss to be a relatively simple matter. We think that if we try to eat less and train more than we have, and feel as though we are 'working hard', that should be enough, the weight will drop off. When this does not happen we become frustrated and annoyed and may even self-sabotage our efforts, thinking, 'Stuff it, why bother, I may as well eat that block of chocolate,' ultimately creating our own cycle of weight loss and regain, month after month, year after year.

There is no doubt that weight loss can be slow and at times frustrating, but if you focus on how hard weight loss is, and are resentful of how hard you have to work to get results, you basically end up fighting a losing battle with your own body, repeating the same diet patterns time and time again. Even more concerning is that we continue to waste our precious energy on these frustrations rather than concentrating on what we need to do, or to alter within the program, to get the weight loss results we are working towards.

There are no hard and fast rules that can ensure continual weight loss for everyone. Each of us has a different metabolic rate, day-to-day schedule and genetic background, and different diet and exercise habits, which means that each and every one of us will respond differently throughout the weight loss process. Myriad things can affect how much weight you lose each week, and micromanaging this loss will ultimately drive you crazy as you try and understand every gram of weight the scales show you lose. Metabolism is so complex and affected by so many different things that the sooner we accept that weight loss is ultimately a longer-term goal and focus on the end point of our plan rather than the weekly intricacies, the sooner we will start to move forward. So if you find yourself frustrated, annoyed and even in despair at any time throughout your weight loss journey, you need to remind yourself of a few thought patterns that must be contained if you are to reach your weight loss goals.

Manage your expectations

If we held no expectations in terms of weight loss, the process would be much easier. Any loss would be a good thing and we would never be frustrated, annoyed or disappointed with a relatively small outcome. The issue is that we all have expectations, whether they have been taught to us, or we have inferred them from other weight loss experiences or advertising claims in the past. As a result of these influences, we often expect weight loss to be easy, or at least to see results when we feel as though we deserve them. We expect to see much greater changes on the scales than the body is even able to physically manage and we expect to see results much more quickly than we ever get them.

If you find yourself constantly disappointed when you check your weight each week, it may indeed be time to alter some of these expectations. Certain phases of weight loss will be hard, especially if we have a large amount of weight to lose. Sometimes we will get results and sometimes we won't, and we need to learn to change our programs to see continual results. We need to expect that what we *expect* will not always be the case, simply because metabolism and weight loss are complicated and still not completely understood. We need to learn to manage our weight loss expectations, and focus on our long-term weight loss goal rather than the week-to-week ups and downs.

Use any result as feedback

So consider a situation in which you have just weighed in and the scales have not budged. Rather than getting distressed about it, try and simply view this result as a time to review what you have been doing. The first thing to ask yourself is whether you would have expected to lose weight given what you have been eating and how much you have been training. If the answer is yes, you then need to consider if there is anything else that may explain this lower than expected result. Have you been eating out a lot or having some extras? Are you training as hard as you could? Have you been eating a lot of salt-rich foods, or are you retaining fluid because you are about to get your period?

In 80 per cent of cases there is some explanation for a 'non-result' on the scales. The other 20 per cent can be explained by the intricacies of weight loss, meaning that in some weeks you will lose weight and in some you won't. Sometimes it takes a bit of time for the body to churn up body fat to burn it, sometimes you may have inflammation or sore muscles which are holding onto extra fluid – there are many reasons why you may not have lost weight this week, and again we could waste much time trying to identify and decipher each one.

Knowing these facts, we then have a choice: we can dwell on a disappointing result, get upset and fail to move forward for another week, or we can get over it, accept that in some weeks we will lose weight and in some weeks we won't, and get on with it. The choice is yours.

Be honest with yourself

At times as a dietitian you have to be honest with clients, and sometimes you have to tell clients gently if they appear to be a little lazy or could make more of an effort. In some cases clients may be eating much more food than they need, or they may just not be taking enough care with their food. At others times there may be a perceived inability or even refusal to exercise, which may have to be interpreted as being lazy and not 100 per cent committed to achieving the stated weight loss goal.

If you know that your personality can result in you being a little slack, a non-result on the scales means that it may be time to get a little more honest. Deep down we all know if we have not been working as hard as we should or have been a little slack with our food. Just because it feels as though you are working, this does not mean that you are. Calorie monitoring and heart rate monitoring while you are training are two good ways of checking if you really are working hard, or simply think you are.

No more whingeing

So you have not lost weight and you are upset, but no one said weight loss was easy, so why on earth would you think or expect it would be? Few things in life are really easy, and yet rather than accept this and move forward we complain, we whinge and we feel sorry for ourselves. This may surprise you, but the reality is that few people are metabolically blessed to the extent that they can eat whatever they like and never gain weight.

One of the most powerful decisions you can make during your weight loss program is to banish self-pity, excuses and complaints from your vocabulary. Whenever you start to complain or whinge, remind yourself that it is helping no one, including yourself, and that the only way to move forward is to be action-driven. Action-driven means focusing only on what you could do right now to help yourself move forward. The sooner you stop wasting your energy on complaining, the sooner you get into the right mindset to move forward and stop holding yourself back, mentally and physically.

Know when there is cause for concern

Some weeks you may drop 2 kilos and others none at all, but if your weight loss is positive over a 2–4 week period and your measurements are dropping, you are on the right track. If, though, you have been eating well and training for 4–6 weeks with no change in weight, then it is time to make some changes. Check out the chapter on plateaus or alter your calorie intake and/or training program to get things moving again. Most importantly, remember your long-term weight loss goal and take each week as it comes. It is all part of the process.

Changing destructive weight loss thoughts

THOUGHT	ALTERNATIVE VIEW
This is so hard.	It may be hard but the results will be worth it.
I thought I would have lost weight.	What could I do differently next week?
Everyone else loses weight so easily.	Everyone who wants to lose weight has to work at it.
But I tried hard.	Trying does not always mean doing the right thing.
It is taking so long.	It will always take longer than you want it to.
I don't know what I did wrong.	Sometimes you don't do anything wrong.

I lost 2 kilos last week.	Sometimes you will lose a lot, sometimes none.
I will never lose weight.	You won't if you think you won't.
I don't know what else to do.	What else could you do?
I think I will gain weight next week.	You will if you give yourself permission to gain.

When you have 6 months

❖ *The exciting thing when you allow 6 months to lose weight is that over that time you will cement habits that will help you control your weight for life.*

If you want to lose 20 or more kilos, you need to allow yourself at least 6 months to achieve this. With the right diet and the right training program, this is a realistic time frame in which to lose this much weight as long as you are able to maintain your focus and motivation. It is easy to get distracted and/or discouraged when weight loss seems to be 'taking so long'. There is also the issue that, having lost weight, you may return to your old habits before you have reached your goal weight. On the flipside, allowing yourself 6 months to reach your goal means that you don't have to be a weight loss purist for weeks and weeks at a time; you can easily lose half a kilo to a kilo a week if you maintain some key dietary changes and a regular training program.

So where do you begin when your goal is to lose more than 20 kilos of weight? You have two choices. You can begin with the plans outlined in the earlier chapters of *Lose Weight Fast* – that is, start with the 3–5 day program, follow with the 1–2 week program, and then move on to the one-month and 3 month plans with the goal of losing at least 10 kilos over the initial 3–4 months. Finally you can move on to the 6 month program. Alternatively, you can commit to a slightly slower but often sustainable approach for the entire 6 months as is outlined in this chapter. In this case you will still lose weight but at the rate of half a kilo to a kilo each week.

Before you start

As with any major project in life, you need to do some planning to give yourself the best chance of succeeding in the long term. Here are a few things to consider before you begin.

HOW AND WHY DID YOU GAIN THE WEIGHT?

If you have 20 or more kilos to lose, a crucial thing to consider before you embark on any new program is how and why you gained so much weight in the first place. For many of us, hectic lives, age, work and relationship demands, combined with a gradual reduction in our metabolic rate, are the key reasons why we gain weight over a number of years. While it does take time to get the body functioning optimally and burning fat efficiently when you have carried extra weight for a number of years, there is no reason why, with appropriate lifestyle changes, you cannot lose your excess weight.

For some people, weight issues may be a little more deep-rooted and need some further exploration. In particular, if you have had weight issues since you were a child, if you have a history of eating disorders, if you have 50 or more kilos to lose, or if you have high insulin or high blood glucose levels, it would be advisable for you to consult a dietitian or a psychologist before you embark on any weight loss program.

Signs you may need some extra help

- You need to lose 50 or more kilos.
- You are suffering from depression or anxiety.
- You have dieted for most of your adult life without success.
- You are following programs but not getting results.
- You have Type 2 diabetes, polycystic ovarian syndrome (PCOS) or insulin resistance. (Insulin resistance is discussed on page 203.)

In these situations, while the general diet and training principles outlined in *Lose Weight Fast* will still apply, sometimes you may need extra support during your weight loss program to keep you on track. Don't be afraid to seek this extra advice and support should you need it.

IDENTIFY WHAT NEEDS TO CHANGE

The factors that have contributed to weight gain will vary from person to person, although there are obviously some common themes. For some of us it will be that we eat too much, for others that we move too little, and for many it will be a combination of the two. It is crucial that you take time to consider exactly which aspects of your current lifestyle need to change – and change in a way that is sustainable in the long term.

You may need to commit to regular personal training, or to change the way you train, to get the results you are looking for. Perhaps you need to see a dietitian regularly to keep you on track. You may need to have some counselling to help you work through some personal issues, or you may need to recruit your husband, wife or partner to work with you. You may need to work shorter hours or hire some extra help at home so you have more time to train regularly. The changes required will be different for each person, but until you consider the changes you personally need to make in the context of your busy life, a new weight loss program will simply be yet another diet you follow for a short period of time before reverting to your old, weight-gaining lifestyle.

START WITH ONE CHANGE AT A TIME

Attempting to make a lot of changes at the one time almost invariably backfires. You will feel overwhelmed, and when everything doesn't come together perfectly (and it won't), you may be left feeling like a failure. To give yourself the best chance of success, focus on making one simple change at a time. For example, you might work on getting your breakfast right one week, and then dinner the following week. This strategy can be particularly useful when it comes to exercise. For people who are not regular exercisers the whole idea can seem daunting. A good way round this is to concentrate on making changes to your eating habits for a few weeks or even months to kick-start your weight loss, and then, when you will be feeling more motivated, to move on to exercise. This can be a great way to lose weight gradually but sustainably over a 6 month period.

FIND THE BALANCE THAT WORKS FOR YOU

While you need to stick to a fairly strict regime to get results in a short time frame and there is no room for extras, you can afford to be a little more flexible when you are looking to lose weight over a 6 month period. For example, some people like to be strict during the week and then take the weekends off. Others like to go in hard in the beginning of a weight loss program and then ease off. And then there are those people who would rather walk for 3 hours a day than go without their daily glass or two of wine.

When we are aiming for a calorie deficit, which means taking in less food energy (calories) than the total calories we use each day, our patterns of food intake tend to have a bigger impact on weight loss than simply aiming for 200–300 calories fewer per day. This means that you are much better off to keep your dinners low in calories for the entire week, or to cut out alcohol for an entire week, than to total up your calories each day and make sure you are under a certain number. The reason for this is that the underlying hormonal regulation of digestion, and ultimately of fat loss, determines which type of fuel you will be burning, and the more tightly controlled we can get this, the more likely we will be effectively burning body fat while maintaining a calorie deficit.

Here are some common lifestyle habits that you may find you need to adjust in order to continue losing weight.

LIFESTYLE HABIT	WEIGHT LOSS HABIT
Drinking alcohol every night.	Drinking 1–2 nights a week.
Having 3–4 drinks a night.	Having just one drink a night.
Eating dessert every night.	Eating dessert once a week.
Eating cake at work 2–3 times a week.	Eating cake at most once a week.
Taking the weekend off your diet.	Taking one meal off.
Not exercising on weekends.	Walking every day.
Eating treats when you have been 'good'.	Eating treats on special occasions.

10 key strategies for your 6 month weight loss program

The strategies for losing weight over 6 months do not differ significantly from those that will support you in losing weight over 3 months. The key difference is knowing that at certain times over a 6 month period you will need to adjust your calorie intake and training habits to allow you to see continual reductions on the scales.

1. GET YOUR CALORIES RIGHT

One of the most difficult aspects of prescribing diets for weight loss is that there is not a standard calorie intake that will work for everyone. Some people will lose weight on a 1500 calorie plan, while others will need just 1200 calories. Then, once you have lost 5–8 kilos on a particular calorie intake, you will most likely need to alter your intake in order to challenge the body's cells and increase metabolic rate over time.

The programs in *Lose Weight Fast* are based on various calorie ranges according to the time frame involved. The 3–5 day and 1–2 week programs are around 1200 calories, while the one-month and 3 month plans are between 1400 calories and 1600 calories. When you set out to lose weight over a 3–6 month time frame, in general you need to aim for at least 1500 calories, but there may be times where you can drop it down to 1200 calories for a week or two if your weight loss has slowed, or even increase it to 1600–1800 calories if you are hungry and training every day.

At the end of the next chapter you will find a range of calorie plans you can try. If you are starting out, try the 1200 calorie plan for a week or two and then, as your weight loss slows, move on to the higher-calorie plans. If you have already worked through *Lose Weight Fast* and used some of the different plans, whether it is from the one-month or three-month plan, and you are losing weight, keep going. If things have slowed, try a higher-calorie or lower-calorie plan for a week or two until you start to lose weight again.

The most important thing to remember is that change is the key when it comes to weight loss over a 3–6 month period, so aim to change your calorie intake every 4–6 weeks.

2. ESTABLISH YOUR KEY FOOD HABITS

Whether you want to lose 2, 10 or 30 kilos and keep it off, there are a number of key food habits you need to develop and maintain for the rest of your life. We often search for the latest and greatest tricks to help us shed weight, but ultimately long-term weight loss comes back to 10 key food habits. Think of these as your 'weight loss commands' and you will never be far off track.

Your 10 key food habits

1. Eat a protein-rich breakfast before 8 am on most days

This is the number one rule of weight loss and long-term weight control. The first meal of the day kick-starts your metabolism to burn calories and the earlier you have it, the better. Including 15–20 grams of protein in your breakfast choice also helps to regulate the hormones that keep you full throughout the day.

Protein-rich breakfasts

2 eggs on 2 slices of wholegrain toast

130 g can of baked beans on 2 slices of wholegrain toast

1 cup of low-fat cottage cheese with 4 corn cakes

1 scoop (20 g) of protein powder with 200 ml skim milk

200 g natural yoghurt with 1 cup of mixed berries and 2 teaspoons of protein powder

⅓ cup oats, or 1 breakfast biscuit, with 200 ml low-fat milk

50 g low-fat ham and 1 slice (20 g) of reduced-fat cheese on 2 slices of wholegrain bread

2. You must eat 3–5 cups of salad and/or vegetables every single day

It sounds like a lot, but only because few of us eat anywhere near this amount. Salad and vegetables are low in calories and also fill us up so that there is basically far less room in our bellies for rubbish. Plus they are packed with nutrients.

3. You must eat dinner by 8 pm on most nights

Late night eating is a recipe for disaster when it comes to weight loss but is unfortunately common in modern life. A good mantra in this situation is, 'The later the dinner, the smaller it needs to be.' If you find yourself routinely eating your main meal after 8 pm, it may be a good idea to start having your biggest meal at lunchtime and then enjoying a light soup or salad later at night. You will find a selection of dinner recipes on pages 157–167. These contain 400–500 calories and 20–30 grams of total carbohydrate.

4. You must give up sugar-based drinks such as fruit juice, soft drink and cordial

Sugar-based drinks, whether fruit or otherwise, should really have no place in anyone's diet, whether or not they are trying to lose weight. They offer nothing nutritionally and so are simply 'empty calories' that the vast majority of us don't compensate for, and they have a high glycemic index, which means they result in relatively high amounts of the hormone insulin being released – the hormone that promotes fat storage in the body.

5. You must snack on a handful of nuts each day

Especially for those wishing to lose weight, nuts offer a number of nutritional benefits, including providing the types of fats that can actually help with fat burning. The key, of course, is being able to stop at just 10–15 or a total of approximately 30 grams.

6. You must limit yourself to 1–2 small skim milk coffees each day

If there is one habit that can play havoc with weight loss it is the consumption of numerous milk-based coffees, such as lattes and cappuccinos, every day. While 1–2 coffees is no issue, continually drinking liquid calories, even if it is coffee, can prevent weight loss.

To avoid this, enjoy your coffee with a meal or as a snack and stick to water or herbal tea in between.

7. You must never leave the house without a protein-rich snack

Planning is the key to dietary success, and never leaving the house without a protein-rich snack ensures that you never get caught out without something nutritious and filling to snack on.

8. You must not overindulge more than once each week

At times we will all eat higher-calorie foods, but the secret to weight loss success is to ensure that this does not happen too often. Aim for no more than one higher-calorie meal or treat each week and you will still be able to lose weight at a good rate (half a kilo to a kilo) without feeling too deprived.

9. You must leave 2–3 hours in between meals and snacks

Leaving a significant amount of time in between eating occasions ensures that you leave enough time to digest all of your food and so allow your natural hunger to govern when you eat a meal or a snack.

10. You must control your dinner portions

Dinner is the most common meal at which we overdo things. Ideally, a dinner meal should be relatively small and fit into just one small bowl apart from the vegetables and/or salad that accompany it. If you know you tend to overdo things at dinner, try serving your dinner in small bowls or on small plates to help regulate your portions.

3. FOCUS ON VEGETABLES

You will have noticed that vegetables have been mentioned numerous times in *Lose Weight Fast*. The reason for this is that the simple act of eating as much salad and vegetables as you can every single day, whether they are raw, dressed, stir-fried or in a soup, is often all that is needed for you to lose weight. When we don't eat the 3–5 cups of vegetables or salad we need, we inevitably eat more of the calorie-dense foods, which makes it harder to control our calorie intake and to lose weight.

At every meal or snack, consider what sort of vegetable and salad bulk you could add. The more you eat, the better it is for weight loss.

4. GET STRAIGHT BACK ON TRACK AFTER A LAPSE

Over a 6 month period of time, there will always be times when life overtakes your efforts to lose weight. You may have a family drama, or a crisis at work, or various demands on your time and energy that mean you are unable to stick to your food and training program 100 per cent. If such events disrupt your routines for a week or two, while you may not lose weight, you should not gain either, as long as you don't make silly food choices within your current constraints.

The key to ensuring that various life events don't undo months of hard work is to get straight back on track as soon as possible when things return to normal. Rather than waiting 'until Monday' or 'starting next week', get into the regular habit of starting the very minute that you can – this way your weight, health and fitness will always be a priority and you will avoid large fluctuations in your weight even when things are not 100 per cent on track.

5. TRAIN EFFECTIVELY

While you may be able to shift 3–5 kilos over a 6–12 week period simply by eating less, at some point during the weight loss process you are going to have to train your body in order to improve your body's ability to burn calories. Unfortunately, when it comes to exercise people tend to be much better at maintaining their current weight than actually training the muscle to work better and burn more calories. Training involves getting your heart rate up 70–80 per cent of its maximum rate (220 minus your age) for at least 30 minutes at least three times per week. While walking may do this for you for the initial 4–6 weeks of your program, eventually your body will get used to this amount of exercise and you will have to change things around and do more, or a different type of training, to keep losing weight.

Some people find it easier to do more, for example to train intensely every day, while others prefer to add extra walking to balance their gym classes or power walks. Others may invest in a personal trainer for a period of time, while there is also the option of doing various exercise programs at home. There is no one style of training, or balance of walking and cardio training, that will suit everyone, but if you are no longer losing weight despite following a calorie-controlled plan, it is usually time for you to change things around.

If cardio training has been your sole focus, you may need to add some resistance training to build muscle tissue, which will in turn help to increase your metabolic rate. For people who have never done resistance training this can seem quite a daunting prospect. Resistance training can include anything from lifting a few hand weights at home, to attending a weights class at the gym, to following a program devised by a personal trainer. If you are already exercising 4–5 times each week and eating calorie-controlled meals and you are still not getting results, this is a sign that you may need to incorporate some resistance training into your workout plan. Doing some form of resistance training 1–2 times each week, or adding 20 minutes of light weights training to a 20–30 minute cardio session, is a great way to reap the benefits of both forms of training in a fairly gentle way.

6. CONTROL AND REDIRECT YOUR THOUGHTS

After weeks if not months of following a weight loss program, you may find that you are battling with mind games and/or negative thoughts that are undermining your weight loss attempts. Negative thought patterns such as 'This week I will be good' or 'I have gone completely off track' or 'I will never lose weight, it is all too hard' are highly likely to send you off the rails and see you returning to the kinds of poor food and training habits that will result in your regaining weight. Such thought patterns are of no help at all and need to be identified as early as possible, challenged and ultimately overcome.

The key is to analyse and challenge such thoughts. For example, the statement 'I have been good' has no meaning – good according to what? Some self-developed rules for eating and exercise? The same can be said for the line 'I have gone off track' – according to what? Simply because you ate a few too many calories on one occasion? Such beliefs and negative thought patterns may have been programmed into our brains for many years by both life experience and what we were taught as children, but actually isolating the exact thought or belief that you have and directly questioning it is often all you need to identify the irrational thought and directly challenge it.

If you find that you are constantly having mind battles that are holding you back, a key strategy for moving forward is to practise redirecting your thoughts to positive actions you can take that will help you achieve your long-term goal. For example, if you routinely justify eating treats because you have done some exercise or have had a hard day, think about what you could do instead that will make you feel better without sabotaging your efforts to lose weight, such as go for a walk, get a massage, or buy some flowers for the house. Or if your thoughts are not rational, for example, 'I am completely off track', focus instead on what you could do from this very minute to get back on track, such as going for a walk or to the gym, or cooking a healthy meal for the week ahead. Shifting thoughts to actions is a powerful strategy to avoid becoming a victim of your own negative thought patterns.

7. RECRUIT YOUR SUPPORT TEAM

It is only natural that our relationships have a powerful influence on how we live our lives, whether they are family relationships, intimate relationships, friendships, or interactions with work colleagues and neighbours. So when we want to make significant lifestyle changes, we need the help and support of at least some of those around us.

When you are planning to make changes to your diet and exercise habits, you may need to have some 'crucial conversations' with the people closest to you – conversations in which you openly discuss what you need from the other person. Sometimes we assume without even asking them that our partner, our children, our best friend or our work colleagues won't be supportive, when in fact they would be happy to help us if we are able to clearly instruct them in terms of what help and support they can provide.

There will always be people in life who get satisfaction out of seeing others fail or proactively making it more difficult for them to succeed. There are also people who are kind and caring and who enjoy helping others to be at their best. As far as possible, we need to steer clear of the former and surround ourselves with the latter.

It will not only help us to achieve our weight loss goals but also contribute to a happier life in general.

8. KEEP GOING WHEN THINGS ARE TOUGH

Having the ability to keep going in the face of adversity is one of the biggest predictors of success in life in general as well as success in losing weight. When you are losing weight over a longer time period, there will be times when you lose a lot and times when you may not lose anything, even though you may have been doing exactly the same thing each week. Responding to disappointing results with resentment, anger and frustration is only likely to make it harder to move forward. In fact, the focus on a lack of results is often counterproductive, because we are focusing on what is not working, and the behaviours we focus on will continue. Sure, there will be times when your progress plateaus, but unless a plateau has continued for several weeks, the best thing you can do is to stay focused, be mindful of the key diet and exercise variables that you need to work on each week, and continue to work towards your long-term weight loss goal.

9. SHIFT FROM MOTIVATION TO ACCEPTANCE

Whenever you see literature on weight loss, you will find numerous tips for keeping motivated. The whole concept of finding and maintaining motivation in turn suggests that if we do not have it, we will not be able to stay on track with our programs, and that it is an ever-elusive state that we must continually search for to be successful.

When it comes to weight loss and weight control we need to shift our focus from the transient state of motivation to one of acceptance – acceptance that eating well and moving our body is something we are going to need to do for the rest of our lives. Shifting this focus frees us from a constant search for motivation and instead concentrating on the basics of what we need to do to keep ourselves on track. It can be all too easy to blame a lack of compliance and even laziness on 'not being motivated', but we are the only person who suffers. Instead, shift your focus to doing rather than 'feeling like doing' and you will find yourself directed rather than 'lacking motivation'.

10. ADJUST YOUR PROGRAMS AS NEEDED

When you are on a longer-term weight loss program, it is most important to adjust your food intake and type of training regularly in order to constantly challenge your body so that you keep losing weight.

To implement this self-review process is easy. Simply allocate time once every week to assess where things are up to with your program. If you have lost weight the week before, it is a sign that you are on the right track. If you haven't, you may need to tighten things up a little. Some of the things you may need to consider are as follows:

➤ **Do you think you should have lost weight given your food and activity levels?**
If so, you may need to increase your calories by 100–200 if your daily intake is just 1200–1400 calories, or cut them by 100–200 calories if your daily intake is between 1400–1600 calories.

➤ **Have you completed your 3–4 training sessions for the week?**
If you haven't, it is time to schedule in your sessions for the week ahead.

If you have, you may need to switch to shorter but more intense sessions in order to burn more calories, or you may need to do different classes or machines for a week or two.

If you have been training alone, it may be worth seeing a personal trainer to revise your program.

Or if you have been training every day, you may need to cut back to just 2–3 sessions a week to give your body a break.

➤ **Have you been doing the amount of walking you need to do?**
Check your pedometer. If you are not clocking up 7500–10,000 steps a day and you have an office job, it is highly likely that your sedentary lifestyle is preventing you from losing as much weight each week as you could be.

Your 6 month weight loss program month by month

Losing a significant amount of weight over a 6 month period is a major achievement, but it is easy to feel a bit discouraged at times when things seem a little slow. A great way to avoid this is to break your weight loss journey down into smaller stages. This enables you to pace yourself and helps you to stay motivated so that you reach your goal weight.

FIRST MONTH
Commit to working solely on your dietary changes. This means preparing healthy foods, eating regularly, and sticking to fairly strict mealtimes and your calorie targets. Focus on eating plenty of vegetables and salad each day, and try taking a month off from drinking alcohol. With these basic changes you should easily lose 2–3 kilos even if your only exercise is simply to start walking regularly. If you are super keen, you can try the Strip Plan for 3–5 days (see page 18), or the 1–2 week plan (see page 34), but remember that these are both strict regimes and should be followed for just 1–2 weeks at most.

MONTHS 2–3

After your initial weight loss, you should be feeling much better about things and have got into a good routine with your food. The important thing is to not get carried away with your progress so far and to keep focused, at most relaxing with just a meal or two each week. Ideally, you should be now walking regularly, and it may also be time to consider some more intensive training options to make sure you keep losing half a kilo to a kilo a week.

MONTHS 4–5

After 3 months of dieting you should be at least 5 kilos lighter, if not closer to 10 kilos, and feeling pretty amazing. At this point you may be getting hungry and so may need to increase your calorie intake by 100–200 calories, particularly during the day, to fuel your body adequately. You are also likely to need to change your training program regularly every 4–6 weeks to ensure that you are continually challenging yourself and losing weight regularly. At this stage you should be able to relax your program a little on weekends, as long as you keep up your training sessions during the week, and still lose half a kilo a week.

MONTH 6

By the 6 month mark you should be feeling like a new person, with at least 10–15 kilos off and hopefully closer to 20 kilos. You will need a new wardrobe and be feeling like you have more energy than you did when you were a teenager. The most important thing now is to understand that the way you are eating and exercising is the way you will eat and exercise for life – it is no longer a program but a way of life, and understanding this will allow you to remain in control of your weight for good.

Sample 6 month food plan

This menu contains an average of 1600–1700 calories per day.

	MONDAY	TUESDAY	WEDNESDAY
BREAKFAST	1 poached egg + 1 slice wholegrain toast + 1 glass tomato juice	1 slice wholegrain toast + 130 g can baked beans + 2 kiwi fruit	⅓ cup oats + 1 cup low-fat milk + 2 kiwi fruit
MID-MORNING	1 piece of fruit	100 g low-fat yoghurt + ½ cup berries	1 piece of fruit
LUNCH	100 g can tuna/salmon + 130 g can mixed beans + mixed salad + 1 tsp olive oil dressing	100 g grilled chicken breast + 1 slice flatbread + mixed salad + 1 tsp olive oil dressing	½ cup brown rice + 95 g can tuna mixed with red capsicum and sweet chilli sauce
MID-AFTERNOON	5 walnuts	10 almonds + 1 apple	2 corn thins + 1 tsp peanut butter
DINNER	100 g piece grilled fish + vegetables stir-fried in 1 tsp olive oil	100 g lean steak fillet + salad	100 g grilled chicken + salad

THURSDAY	FRIDAY	SATURDAY	SUNDAY
1 poached egg + 1 slice wholegrain toast + 1 glass tomato juice	1 slice wholegrain toast + 130 g can baked beans + 2 kiwi fruit	⅓ cup oats + 1 cup low-fat milk + 2 kiwi fruit	2 poached eggs + 2 slices wholegrain toast
100 g low-fat yoghurt + ½ cup berries	1 piece of fruit	100 g low-fat yoghurt + ½ cup berries	1 piece of fruit
100 g can tuna/salmon + 130 g can mixed beans + mixed salad + 1 tsp olive oil dressing	100 g grilled chicken breast + 1 slice flatbread + mixed salad	Jacket potato topped with 100 g red salmon + ⅓ cup cottage cheese + tomato	100 g lean beef strips + 2 flatbread wraps + salad
1 piece of fruit	2 corn thins + thin spread avocado	15 almonds	5 walnuts
100 g piece grilled fish + vegetables stir-fried in 1 tsp olive oil	100 g lean lamb + vegetables	100 g tuna fillet with Asian vegetables	Vegetable soup + 100 g grilled Atlantic salmon

Sample 1400–1500 calorie plan

	MONDAY	TUESDAY	WEDNESDAY
BREAKFAST	2 poached eggs + 2 slices wholegrain toast	1 slice wholegrain toast + 130 g can baked beans	2 poached eggs + 2 slices wholegrain toast
MID-MORNING	1 piece of fruit	Protein shake in skim milk	100 g low-fat yoghurt + ½ cup mixed berries
LUNCH	100 g can tuna/salmon + 130 g can mixed beans + 130 g can corn + mixed salad + 1 tsp olive oil dressing	100 g grilled chicken breast + 2 slices flatbread + mixed salad + 1 tsp olive oil dressing	¾ cup brown rice + 95 g can tuna mixed with 1 tbsp sweet chilli sauce
MID-AFTERNOON	10 walnuts + 100 g low-fat yoghurt	15 almonds	2 corn thins + 2 tsp peanut butter + 1 apple
DINNER	150 g piece grilled fish + piece sweet potato + vegetables stir-fried in 1 tsp olive oil	150 g lean steak fillet + 1 small baked potato + salad	150 g grilled chicken + 1 baked potato + salad

THURSDAY	FRIDAY	SATURDAY	SUNDAY
⅓ cup oats + 1 cup low-fat milk + 2 kiwi fruit	2 poached eggs + 2 slices wholegrain toast	⅓ cup oats + 1 cup low-fat milk + 2 kiwi fruit	2 poached eggs + 2 slices wholegrain toast
Protein shake skim milk + berries	100 g low-fat yoghurt + [½ cup??] mixed berries	1 piece of fruit	Protein shake skim milk
100 g can tuna/ salmon + 1 slice flatbread + mixed salad + 1 tsp olive oil dressing	100 g grilled chicken breast + 2 pieces flatbread + mixed salad	Jacket potato topped with red salmon + ⅓ cup cottage cheese + tomato + 1 piece of fruit	100 g lean beef strips + 2 flat bread wraps + salad 2 slices flatbread
1 piece of fruit	2 corn thins + thin spread avocado + 1 apple	15 almonds + glass skim milk	10 walnuts
150 g piece grilled lamb + baked sweet potato + vegetables stir fried in 1 tsp olive oil	150 g chicken breast + ½ cup brown rice + stir-fried vegetables in oyster sauce	150 g tuna steak on sweet potato mash + Asian greens	Vegetable soup + 150 g grilled Atlantic salmon

Sample 1800 calorie plan

	MONDAY	TUESDAY	WEDNESDAY
BREAKFAST	2 poached eggs + 2 slices wholegrain toast + 1 orange	2 slices wholegrain toast + 130 g can baked beans + 2 slices reduced-fat cheese	2 poached eggs + 2 slices wholegrain toast + 1 orange
MID-MORNING	1 piece fruit + 150 g low-fat yoghurt	Protein shake + 200 ml skim milk + ½ banana	1 piece fruit + 150 g low-fat yoghurt
LUNCH	150 g can tuna/salmon + wholegrain bread roll + mixed salad + ¼ avocado	100 g grilled chicken breast + 1 piece wholemeal Lebanese bread + mixed salad	1 cup cooked brown rice + 100 g can tuna mixed with ½ red capsicum and sweet chilli sauce
MID-AFTERNOON	Nut-based bar	15 almonds + 1 piece fruit	4 corn thins + thin spread peanut butter
DINNER	200 g grilled fish + 1 jacket potato + vegetables stir-fried in 1 tsp olive oil	200 g lean fillet steak + 1 small baked potato + salad	200 g grilled chicken + ¾ cup cooked brown rice + stir-fried vegetables

THURSDAY	FRIDAY	SATURDAY	SUNDAY
½ cup oats + 1 cup low-fat milk + 1 orange	2 slices wholegrain toast + 130 g can baked beans + 2 slices reduced-fat cheese	½ cup oats + 1 cup low-fat milk + 2 kiwi fruit or ½ cup berries	2 poached eggs + 2 slices wholegrain toast
Protein shake skim milk + ½ cup berries	1 glass low-fat milk + 2 corn cakes + 2 tsp peanut butter	1 piece fruit	Protein shake 200 ml skim milk + ½ cup berries
100 g can tuna/salmon + 130 g can mixed beans + 1 piece flatbread + mixed salad + 1 tsp olive oil dressing	150 g grilled chicken breast + 1 slice flatbread + mixed salad	Jacket potato topped with red salmon + ⅓ cup cottage cheese + tomato + 100 g yoghurt or 1 piece fruit	150 g lean beef strips + 2 pieces flatbread + salad
1 piece fruit + 15 nuts	2 corn thins + thin spread avocado + 1 piece fruit	Nut-based bar	10–15 nuts
200 g grilled fish + vegetables stir-fried in 1 tsp olive oil	200 g lamb fillet + 1 baked sweet potato + vegetables	200 g tuna fillet + Asian greens on ¾ cup cooked brown rice	Vegetable soup + 200 g grilled Atlantic salmon

RECIPES FOR YOUR 6 MONTH PLAN

The recipes in this section range from 400 calories to 500 calories and are good dinner options to support weight loss when you are 3–6 months into your program.

CHICKEN AND MUSHROOM FILO PARCELS

1 tablespoon olive oil

1 onion, finely chopped

2 cloves garlic, crushed

300 g button mushrooms, chopped

400 g chicken breast fillets, chopped

375 ml can light evaporated milk

8 sheets filo pastry

Canola oil spray

4 cups mixed snow peas, beans, broccoli

1 Heat half the oil in a large pan. Add onion, garlic and mushrooms; cook, stirring, until onion is soft. Transfer to a small bowl.

2 Heat remaining oil in the same pan. Add chicken; cook, stirring, until browned. Stir in milk; simmer, uncovered, for 20 minutes, until sauce is reduced and thickened.

3 Preheat the oven to 180°C. Layer two sheets of filo, spraying between each layer with a little oil. Spoon one-quarter of the chicken mixture along one short end of each double sheet of filo. Fold in the sides, then roll up to enclose filling. Place parcels, seam-side down, on a greased oven tray. Spray lightly with oil and cook in the oven for about 20 minutes, or until lightly browned.

4 Serve with steamed greens.

Serves 4

LOW-FAT GREEN CURRY

750 g chicken breast, finely sliced

2 teaspoons canola or olive oil

2 tablespoons green curry paste

375 g can low-fat coconut evaporated milk

Green beans (1 cup or 100 g)

Broccoli florets

1 red capsicum, sliced

100 g can water chestnuts

2 tablespoons fish sauce

2 tablespoons brown sugar

1 tablespoon cornflour

2 tablespoons water

2 cups cooked brown rice

1 Brown chicken in a pan with a little oil, then add curry paste.

2 Add evaporated milk and bring to the boil, then reduce heat.

3 Add vegetables and water chestnuts and simmer until vegetables are lightly cooked. Add fish sauce and brown sugar.

4 Mix cornflour with 2 tablespoons of water and add to the mixture; stir until curry thickens.

5 Serve with cooked rice.

Serves 4

MANGO CHICKEN

Olive or canola oil spray

2 chicken breasts

425 g can sliced mango

¾ cup water

1 tablespoon soy sauce

1 teaspoon sesame oil

2 tablespoons white vinegar

2 teaspoons sugar

2 chicken stock cubes

2 teaspoons cornflour

1 large red capsicum, sliced

1 piece broccoli, sliced into florets

8 green onions, sliced diagonally into 1 cm pieces

2 cups cooked brown rice

1 Lightly spray pan with oil and brown the chicken breasts. Cut mango into thin slices.

2 Combine water, soy sauce, sesame oil, vinegar, sugar, crumbed stock cubes and cornflour. Add to chicken and cook for a few minutes; then simmer for 5–10 minutes until chicken is cooked through.

3 Add mango, capsicum, broccoli and green onions; heat until broccoli is lightly cooked.

4 Serve with brown rice.

Serves 4

FRENCH ONION CHICKEN

200 g sweet potato, cut into quarters, peeled and boiled

1 cup mushrooms, sliced

2 teaspoons olive oil

1 teaspoon fresh or dried herbs of choice

500 g lean chicken breast, sliced

1 medium-size oven bag

1 packet of French onion soup mix

½ cup water

16 cherry tomatoes, halved

Chives to garnish

1 Lightly steam sweet potato; place on a baking tray with mushrooms and drizzle with olive oil. Sprinkle potato with your favourite seasoning or herbs; bake at 200ºC for 10–15 minutes until cooked and lightly browned.

2 Place chicken in the oven bag; add French onion soup mix and shake well to coat. Add the water and seal the bag. Pierce the bag three times at the top below the tie point to provide ventilation. Place the bag in a microwave oven and cook for 15 minutes on high.

3 Take care when removing the bag from the microwave and also when opening it as a lot of steam will be released. Serve the chicken, sweet potato and mushrooms while hot. Garnish with cherry tomatoes and chives.

Serves 4

CHEESY VEGIES

500 g cauliflower, cut into small florets

500 g broccoli, cut into small florets

2 teaspoons olive oil

1 onion, finely chopped

1 clove garlic, finely chopped

2 pieces 97% fat-free bacon

¼ cup flour

2½ cups low-fat milk

¾ cup reduced-fat cheese

1 Lightly steam cauliflower and broccoli. Place in a baking dish.

2 Heat oil in a saucepan; add onion, garlic and bacon and cook until onion is soft. Add flour and cook over low heat for 2–3 minutes. Add milk and bring to the boil; reduce heat and stir until mixture is thick. Stir in cheese and remove from heat.

3 Pour the sauce over the vegetables in the dish and place in a hot oven (200ºC) until heated through.

Serves 4 as a side dish

SALMON AND RICOTTA TART

Cooking oil spray

4 sheets filo pastry

200 g smoked salmon, roughly chopped

150 g low-fat ricotta

3 tablespoons finely chopped dill

2 eggs, lightly beaten

½ cup low-fat milk

1 Preheat the oven to 180°C. Coat a 20 cm loose-based tart tin with cooking oil spray. Line the base with a sheet of pastry and lightly coat it with cooking oil spray, then place the next sheet of pastry on top. Continue to do this with the remaining pastry sheets. Place on a baking sheet and bake for 8 minutes, until lightly golden.

2 Place the remaining ingredients in a bowl and mix to combine, seasoning well with salt and pepper. Gently pour salmon mixture into the cooked pastry case.

3 Reduce the oven temperature to 160°C and bake for 35 minutes or until the salmon filling is set. Serve with salad.

Serves 4

SPINACH PIE

2 bags or 3–4 cups baby
spinach leaves

2 eggs

250 g low-fat ricotta

200 g reduced-fat fetta

180 g can tuna in water,
drained

2 green onions, chopped

Olive oil spray

4 sheets filo pastry

1 Lightly cook spinach leaves in water in microwave and chop coarsely.

2 Mix together eggs, ricotta, fetta, tuna and chopped onions.

3 Spray a medium-size casserole dish with olive oil and fill with the tuna and cheese mixture.

4 Top with filo and bake at 180°C for 30 minutes or until cooked through and pastry is browned. Serve with a large green salad.

Serves 4

HIGH-PROTEIN LUNCH SALAD

1 Roma tomato

1 Lebanese cucumber

130 g can four bean mix

¼ Spanish onion, finely chopped

1 stick celery, finely chopped

Large bowl mixed rocket and baby spinach

15 walnuts

1 teaspoon honey

1 teaspoon olive oil

1 cup roasted pumpkin

100 g lean lamb or chicken strips

Mix all ingredients together for a filling lunch or dinner salad.

SWEET AND SOUR PORK

Canola oil spray

1 kg lean pork fillet, cut into thin strips

1 onion, sliced

1 small red capsicum, chopped

1 small green capsicum, chopped

1 carrot, sliced

440 g can pineapple pieces, drained (reserve juice)

¼ cup tomato sauce

1 tablespoon chilli sauce

2 cloves garlic, finely chopped

2 tablespoons white vinegar

1 tablespoon cornflour

1 Spray a pan or wok with canola oil. Cook pork for 2–3 minutes over high heat until browned; set aside.

2 Stir-fry onion until lightly browned. Add capsicum and carrot and stir-fry until tender.

3 Place pineapple juice, tomato sauce, chilli sauce, garlic, vinegar and cornflour in a bowl and whisk until smooth.

4 Return pork to wok; add sauce and pineapple pieces, and stir until mixture thickens.

Serves 4

LIGHT SHEPHERD'S PIE

1 large brown onion, finely chopped

1 tablespoon olive oil

500 g best-quality lean mince

2 carrots, diced

2 tablespoons tomato sauce

2 tablespoons HP sauce

2 teaspoons Worcestershire sauce

1 cup frozen peas

2 large, unwashed potatoes

2 cups chopped pumpkin

½ cup reduced-fat grated tasty cheese

1 Fry onion in olive oil until translucent and soft. Add mince and fry until all meat is browned. Drain off any excess fat.

2 Add carrot and sauces to taste (more or less if you wish). Simmer for about 5 minutes and then add frozen peas. Combine the vegetable mixture and the mince and place in a 6 cup casserole or lasagne dish.

3 Boil potato and pumpkin until tender. Mash potato and pumpkin separately and then mix together. Top the meat with the potato mixture, using a fork to spread the topping evenly. Sprinkle with tasty cheese.

4 Bake at 180ºC for about 20 minutes. Serve with a large side salad.

Serves 4–6

MOROCCAN CHICKEN

500 g chicken thigh, skin removed, trimmed of fat

Salt and pepper to taste

Olive oil

2 zucchinis

240 g can chickpeas

1 cup reduced-salt chicken stock

420 g can salt-reduced diced tomatoes

½ teaspoon paprika

1 teaspoon cumin

1 teaspoon cinnamon

2 cups cooked brown rice

1 Season raw chicken with salt and pepper; fry in a small amount of olive oil over medium heat until chicken is lightly browned.

2 Add chopped zucchinis to pan; simmer until soft. Add chickpeas, stock, tomatoes and spices to pan; simmer until cooked through.

3 Serve with cooked brown rice.

Serves 4

Tips and tricks for your 6 month program

- Set aside just half an hour each week, ideally on a Monday morning over a cup of coffee, to plan your meals and snacks in advance – remember, planning is the key to dietary success. You will be less tempted to pick up takeaway each week or to raid the vending machine if you have the foods you need to eat on hand.

- Once you have been dieting for longer than 3 months, it is important to give your body a break from calorie restriction. Neurobiological research has shown that a diet too low in calories can stimulate appetite. To avoid excessive hunger, try having a meal or two off your diet each week, where you eat what you feel like.

- Are you experiencing sugar cravings? If you are, it may mean that you are not consuming the right mix of carbohydrates and proteins. If you need a 4 pm hit, it might be worth adding some more lean protein, such as lean meat, chicken or fish, or low-fat dairy, to your lunch. While it is normal to need a snack mid-afternoon, a huge need for sugar is not, and usually means that something is lacking in your diet.

- Never go to a function or party starving. It is a recipe for disaster. Instead, enjoy a protein-rich snack of thick yoghurt or nuts an hour before you leave to take the edge off your hunger. This will help prevent you from overindulging in high-fat nibbles and bread.

- Each and every time you intend to eat something, ask yourself, 'What do I really feel like eating?' Then commit to only eating foods that you really, really want and enjoy. A lot of times dieters force themselves to eat foods they don't enjoy. By asking this question, you tap into your body's natural hunger and satiety signals and will avoid feeling deprived, as you may on many diets.

- A significant proportion of calories are eaten mindlessly – in front of the television or computer. Commit to only eating sitting down at the table with the television switched off. Chew each mouthful 20 times and put your knife and fork down in between each mouthful. Not only will you eat up to 25 per cent less, you will also enjoy the process of eating more.

- If you don't love it, don't eat it. Life is too short to eat poor-quality food. Choose the best-quality cheese, chocolate, yoghurt and fruits that you can. Avoid highly processed, 97% fat-free cakes and biscuits and artificially sweetened foods, and notice how much better you feel when you are eating something because you really like it as opposed to thinking you 'should' be eating it.

- Check your fats. Although there are 'good fats', the ones we all need for optimal functioning, the amount of these fats we need is very small (approximately 40–60 grams each day for most adults). Foods that supply these good fats but that are commonly overeaten include:

FOOD	FAT CONTENT
Avocado	30 g per half
Nuts	30 g per 50 g (about 20 nuts)
Olive oil	20 g per tbsp
Salmon	20 g per 200 g
Hummus	20 g per ½ cup

6 month weight loss snack list

200 g Greek style yoghurt + 1 piece of fruit

4 wholegrain crackers with 2 slices of fat-reduced cheese

Nut-based snack bar + small skim coffee

Small (50 g) tub of hummus + cut-up vegetables + 20 g reduced-fat cheese

Small skim coffee + 1 piece of fruit

30 g trail mix + small skim coffee

4 corn crackers with 2 teaspoons of peanut butter

20 g dark chocolate + 1 piece of fruit

Mountain bread wrap with ham and 20 g reduced-fat cheese

6 month weight loss checklist

1. Get your calories right.
2. Establish your key food habits.
3. Focus on vegetables.
4. Get straight back on track after a lapse.
5. Train effectively.
6. Control and redirect your thoughts.
7. Recruit your support team.
8. Keep going when things are tough.
9. Shift from motivation to acceptance.
10. Adjust your programs as needed.

When other factors need to be considered

Perhaps the most important thing any of us can do when we are embarking on a serious, long-term weight loss program is to spend some time reflecting on our patterns of behaviour in relation to food and exercise and to try and gain some understanding of why we think and behave the way we do – especially when things are not going as well as we may like. Too often, we put such issues into the 'too hard box' and avoid confronting them. We give the problem a label like 'emotional eating' or 'not being mindful' and say it is a symptom of our stressed lives, but we refuse to own it. Once we start to identify some of the negative thought processes and behaviours that are holding us back, we are in a better position to take responsibility for them and to work towards changing them. Ultimately, regardless of how much weight we want to lose, this is what we all need to do to take charge and move forward in the long term when it comes to any change in behaviour.

There are many issues that could account for someone being unable to lose weight successfully, but the following are among the most common: early childhood programming in regard to food, deeply entrenched habits, low mood and poor self-regulatory skills. Indeed, you could spend years in therapy exploring these issues in depth, but many people are also able to explore them at some level on their own to gain insight into their patterns of behaviour and change them for the better.

Childhood programming

Your parents may have made you eat everything on your plate, or your mother may always have called you fat. You may not have had enough to eat as a child, or you may have felt deprived of treats and now find you cannot stop yourself from eating them. The experiences we have as children are known to be the most powerful programmers of our long-term patterns of behaviour. The way our parents taught us to eat and exercise, and even the way they spoke about food, health and nutrition, often continues to influence our thinking and our habits well into adulthood.

While we can reflect on this, and even blame our parents for some of the ways in which we habitually behave, at some stage we have to take responsibility for ourselves and try to move forward. At times we need to remind ourselves that most parents try to do their best, and if yours managed to impart less than ideal food-related habits on you, this is most likely because they believed at the time that they were doing the right thing. So if you still feel you have to eat everything on your plate, or you devour the entire packet of biscuits because you felt constantly restricted as a child and now there is no longer anyone to stop you, it is time to challenge these beliefs and behavioural patterns.

Here are some common eating habits that may have been formed in childhood. Do any of these sound familiar?

- Feeling you have to eat everything on your plate

- Always having something sweet with a cup of tea or coffee

- Always having dessert

- Not stopping until you have eaten the entire packet of biscuits or chocolates

- Hiding foods you regard as treats

- Restricting treats and then bingeing on them

- Not being able to skip a meal

- Eating not because you are hungry but because it is mealtime

- Resorting to quick meals such as toast or cereal when you are tired

- Comforting yourself with food when you feel down

- Viewing exercise as a chore

Simply becoming aware of these patterns of behaviour is often all you need to start to understand their origins and make the decision to challenge them. While it will take time to shift lifelong habits, it can also be liberating to gain the understanding that the reason we do many of the things we do is not necessarily because we are lazy, greedy or 'unable to control' ourselves but because as children we were taught to behave in this way.

Deeply entrenched habits

The patterns of behaviour we learn in childhood are one thing, but the day-to-day habits that we fall into over months if not years can be more challenging to shift. We human beings are creatures of habit; we tend to like to do the same things, at the same time, each day, each week, and each year. Unfortunately, when it comes to metabolism, eating and exercising the exact same way every day or every week is one of the worst things that we can do. For example, eating the exact same breakfast at the same time every single day does not challenge the cells to burn as efficiently as they could. And when it comes to calorie intake, habits such as stopping to pick up a coffee and banana bread on the way to work each day, or pouring yourself a glass of wine as soon as you walk in the door after a long day, translate into too many extra calories on a daily basis.

There is no quick way of breaking a habit, and we need to allow ourselves at least 3 months to do so. We first need to understand how it is undermining our weight loss efforts and what we could do instead that would help us reach our goal. This is the crucial first step, as it is human nature to revert to old, familiar habits if we are not constantly focusing on the new habits that are to replace them. Then we simply have to practise, practise, practise replacing the old habit with the new one we are working to instil.

Throughout your weight loss process, try and focus on just one habit that needs changing at a time and don't tackle another until you feel that the new habit is now so much a part of your life that you rarely even need to think about it. If we try and change too many things at once, we are likely to end up back where we started just a few days or weeks later.

10 key weight control habits for your 6 month program

1. Eating breakfast before 8 am
2. Doing some physical activity every single day
3. Compensating when you have overeaten
4. Always carrying a protein-rich snack with you
5. Eating 3–4 cups of salad or vegetables every day
6. Enjoying treats in moderation
7. Getting back on track immediately after a blow-out
8. Keeping dinner small
9. Having 3–4 alcohol-free days each week
10. Cooking a low-calorie healthy meal each week to have on hand

Low mood

Low mood is surprisingly common and can have more impact on your weight and health in the long term than you might imagine. If you are feeling unhappy about your life, your work and/or your relationships, it is going to be difficult to focus on making the changes you need to make to lose weight unless you are also working towards improving these other areas of your life. It is not uncommon to see people who have been struggling dreadfully with their weight take control completely once they get other areas of their life on track.

Similarly, it is always important when you are losing weight to keep a sense of perspective and not to neglect other areas of your life. This means not obsessing 100 per cent of the time about what you should and should not be eating but rather keeping busy with other things you enjoy doing. Once you work towards achieving this balance, you will find you have less time to be thinking about food and things naturally fall into place around your basic diet and exercise structure.

To work towards this balance, aim to:

- Schedule regular social outings with friends and family

- Link walks and other exercise to your social activities

- Identify at least one hobby or pastime you enjoy and allocate time to it each week

- Spend time in the sunlight every single day

- Avoid being at home during the times when you are most vulnerable to eat extras, whether it is after dinner or in the late afternoon

Poor self-regulatory skills

❖ *The most important question to ask when it comes to being able to self-regulate eating behaviour is, 'Am I really hungry?'*

It often surprises people to hear that it is human nature to eat when food is in front of them, and since food tends to be around us all the time in modern life, we have to learn to self-regulate if we are to avoid gaining weight. Signs that you may need to work on your self-regulatory skills include not being able to say no if food is in front of you, often eating the entire packet of nuts or biscuits once you open them, constantly overeating when out to dinner or at functions, and eating simply because it is there rather than because you are hungry.

We all find it difficult to self-regulate at times, but if this is an ongoing, almost daily issue for you, it is time to take control. For most of us, learning to self-regulate our food intake comes down to two things: being able to identify when we are hungry and being able to say no when appropriate. Much like the parent of a wayward child, we sometimes have to say no firmly many, many times to get the result we are looking for. Funnily enough though, once you start to say no to the extra slice of cake, the biscuit at work or the extra glass of wine, you will notice that it soon becomes much easier.

10 tips to help you self-regulate your food intake

1. Identify whether you are really hungry before accepting any food.
2. Consider what would be a reasonable portion if you do need to eat.
3. Never go to a party or function hungry.
4. Never stand near the food.
5. Practise not eating what you are served immediately.
6. Aim to never have more than one of anything extra or treat-like.
7. Learn to feel comfortable saying no.
8. Share treats where possible.
9. Practise opening a packet of nuts or biscuits and not eating all of it.
10. Develop firm rules about when you should and should not be eating.

Examples of self-regulatory food rules

1. I only eat dessert once a week.
2. I always share dessert.
3. I never eat if I am not hungry.
4. I only enjoy treats on special occasions.
5. I do not eat cake or chocolate during the day.
6. I eat well during the week so I can relax on weekends.
7. I do not drink alcohol during the week.
8. I can enjoy one biscuit or chocolate but no more.
9. I only eat it if I really feel like it.
10. I don't eat just because everyone else is eating or wants me to eat.

❖ *Ideally, we need to rid ourselves of the thought, 'I deserve it.' The best response to this attempt at justification is, 'Why?'*

Challenging situations

✤ *'I was going so well, and then it was my birthday, followed by two farewells at work, and now I am completely off track.'*

Time after time social occasions and other challenging situations send diet and exercise regimes into complete disarray. Weeks of hard work can be undone in a matter of days as we quickly revert to old behavioural patterns. There is no doubt that a change of environment does make eating well and exercising a little harder, but it does not make it impossible, and this is the first thing to deeply entrench into your psyche if you are to take control of your weight in the long term.

Eating out, special occasions and holidays are often seen as an excuse as well as an opportunity to eat, drink and do whatever we like. If we holidayed once a year and ate out only occasionally this would not be an issue, but the reality is that for most of us there are several holidays a year and multiple social occasions each week, which ultimately means far too many eating and drinking occasions regularly scheduled into the diary to be 'treating' ourselves at every single one.

Eating out

The average takeaway or restaurant meal can contain up to double the number of calories of a meal you would prepare at home. If this surprises you, once you consider the way the food is cooked and the extra bread, oil and sauces that usually come with it, as well as the entrees, desserts and coffees that are often part of a restaurant meal, you will soon see how even your steak and salad can represent a calorie overload when prepared restaurant-style. If you eat out more than once a week and you are serious about losing weight, you are going to have to pull back and make smart choices. Here are your 5 rules.

1. NEVER GO TO A RESTAURANT STARVING

Arriving at your favourite restaurant starving means that you are much more likely to overeat. Take the edge off your appetite by having a protein-rich snack such as a protein or nut bar, a protein shake, or vegetable sticks and hummus an hour or two before you go out, and you will then be in a much better position to make good decisions when it comes to what you order and what you say no to.

2. KNOW YOUR HIGH-CALORIE TRAPS

On any menu, there are certain foods that have to become a 'no go' zone when you are losing weight. Deep-fried food, chips, risotto, creamy pasta, pizza, Asian noodles and desserts are all foods that are going to give you an extra 300–500 calories and blow your weight loss out the window. You will be able to eat out and still lose weight if you choose dishes that are as low in calories as possible.

3. GET THE BALANCE RIGHT

It doesn't matter whether you need to lose 2 kilos or 20 kilos, if you focus on dishes that consist mainly of protein and vegetables you won't go too far wrong – grilled fish and vegetables, chicken stir-fry with no rice, sashimi and beans. While such dishes may not seem as exciting as the fattier, higher-calorie options, just remember that you are losing weight.

4. ORDER EXTRA VEGETABLES

One of the biggest issues with meals you eat away from home is that they rarely have the volume of salad and vegetables you need to get the right balance in your meals. This means that if you need to spend $10 on a plate of steamed vegetables to go with your $30 steak, so be it, as you need at least 2–3 cups of salad or vegetables with your main meal.

5. SHARE, SHARE, SHARE

If there is one trick for eating out that will serve you well for the rest of your life, it is to learn the art of sharing. If you share your meals – for example, eat half a serve of tomato-based pasta with salad rather than a whole serve – you will virtually eliminate the risk of gaining weight from eating out. And once you start to share, you will wonder how you ever managed to eat entire serves.

Dealing with functions and events

❧ *It was so hard. There was nothing decent to eat, so I had to have four little quiches and four sausage rolls because I was starving.'*

Of all the excuses you might come up with, becoming a victim of your food environment is one of the weakest. In all honesty, how many times do you attend a function where low-calorie, low-fat canapés and snacks are served? Never.

If you have committed to losing weight, you need to accept that there will be many occasions when the kind of food you need to eat will not be provided. For this reason, you always need to be prepared and to have a back-up plan. It doesn't matter whether you take your own food with you, use meal replacements or protein bars before you go, or make the decision not to eat at functions. The important thing is to find the strategy that works for you.

Among the foods commonly served at functions, salads, grilled dishes, and light canapés such as sushi, grilled meat skewers and vegetable-based snacks are examples of acceptable choices. Limit the number of small canapés that you consume to just 3–5 at any one function and manage your appetite by having a meal replacement or protein shake before you arrive at the function so you are not hungry; this will make it much easier to control your intake of high-fat snacks.

At work

If you work in a food-filled office environment, you need to take extra care. The biscuits, cakes and confectionery that may be handed around freely, the chocolate at 3 pm and the frequent birthday cakes translate into extra calories on most days of the week and are ultimately the difference between losing weight and not losing. Bad food habits formed at work can be among the most challenging to break, as this is the place where we are likely to find ourselves bored or frustrated, and where we may be subject to peer pressure to eat every single day. No tricks here, just a repeated 'No thank you' said clearly and firmly.

Travelling

Instead of seeing travelling as challenging when it comes to your food intake and training, try looking at it as a major opportunity to be more active and to be in complete control of your food intake. For example, when you find yourself with a three-hour stopover at an airport, if you consider that the terminal is about a kilometre long, by walking up and down it 10 times you clock up an easy 10 kilometres. If you find yourself hungry, since you have planned ahead and packed a shake and can easily grab a coffee or a nut bar at the airport, there is a far lower chance that you will be tempted by the high-fat foods that are usually available.

Whether it is an overnight trip or an overseas holiday, when you are taking a break from your regular schedule you usually have a little more time to be active and also the time to seek out the food you need to eat well. You may eat a little more, but you should also be more active. If you give yourself permission to gain weight simply because you are travelling, you will, but if you look for opportunities to eat better and move more, you will continue to lose weight.

Friends who encourage you to eat

Generally speaking, people feel more comfortable about eating if others around them are eating as well. This means that if one of your friends is keen to indulge in some cake, she is likely to want you to join her.

When you find yourself constantly confronted with this situation, tell your friend that you need her support in your quest to lose weight. This is much more sensible than to constantly have to avoid her or to say no to treats and temptations. If she still pressures you to eat, spend a little less time with her, particularly if you usually get together over food.

Coffee dates

The coffee culture we live in can very easily lead to overeating. One coffee will often turn into two, and coffee is all too often teamed with sweet treats, including cakes, biscuits, banana bread and puddings. While there is nothing wrong with a coffee here or there, numerous milk-based coffees consumed in one sitting along with extra snacks will disrupt your weight loss efforts.

Keep on track by limiting yourself to just one small coffee, and if you must eat at the time, look for a lower-calorie biscuit or biscotti. Better still, eat before you go and sip on a green tea for almost no calories.

The dreaded weight loss 'plateau'

❁ *'I have tried everything – eating less, exercising more – and nothing seems to be working. The scales haven't budged for weeks.'*

Anyone who has been on a weight loss program will know that there is nothing more frustrating than a weight loss plateau, especially after putting in months and months of hard work to get where you are. If you have more than 10 kilos to lose, it is completely normal to experience plateaus from time to time throughout your weight loss program. This happens for a number of physiological reasons. The key things you need to know are how to identify a true plateau and what to change within your diet and training program to get things moving again.

Generally speaking, a plateau occurs during the weight loss process simply because your body likes to keep weight stable. So, if you have lost a significant amount of weight, which may be anywhere between 5 and 10 kilos, your metabolism will start to slow down in order to conserve energy and keep the body at this new weight. This means that if you continue with the same training and calorie intake over a number of weeks, you may find that your weight is not dropping as quickly as it did when you began your program.

Different people will experience plateau at different times, depending on how much weight they have to lose, how much exercise they are doing, and how low they have dropped their calories.

Ultimately, the way to overcome a weight loss plateau is to change things around. In order to continually increase your metabolic rate and optimise your body's ability to burn calories, you need to be constantly challenging your cells with different amounts of food and different ratios of carbs and proteins, and by eating at different times. You also need to vary the types of training you do so that you are utilising different muscle groups for different periods of time. And you need to keep mixing these elements up throughout your weight loss process.

How to identify a plateau

When you think you may be experiencing a weight loss plateau, you need to determine if that is really the case. When you are losing weight over a longer period of time, such as 3–6 months, while you may have been able to lose relatively high amounts of weight initially, say 1–2 kilos a week, in general this rate will slow from time to time during the course of your weight loss program. You will have noticed that in some weeks you lose a good amount of weight, while in others, none. Naturally, the rate of weight loss will slow the closer you get to your goal weight, but it also takes time for fat to be mobilised from the body and taken into the muscles to be burnt. If you can envisage 'churning it up' to burn, then this is more or less what is happening when you are mobilising fat, especially if you have been carrying it for some time. So just because you have not lost weight for a week or two, this doesn't mean you are experiencing a weight loss plateau. For you to truly be experiencing a weight loss plateau, your weight loss needs to have stalled for at least 3 weeks, with no other factors such as a higher calorie intake or less training possibly contributing to the situation.

Check your calories

The most common reason that people plateau is that they have kept their calorie intake too low for too long. While this approach may have worked initially to shift 5 or even 10 kilos, the body is now basically so sick and tired of running on so few calories that it is refusing to run on even fewer. Cutting calories back further is only likely to make the issue worse. If you have tried this, you would have noticed that you are not feeling overly hungry either, as the body is slowing everything down to conserve energy.

If you think your calorie intake may be a little low, or if you have been eating exactly the same thing for weeks on end, basically you need to change things around. Estimate your calorie intake via an online calorie-counting computer program such as CalorieKing. If your calories are below 1000 on an average day, this is undoubtedly why you are not losing weight. Even if they are just on the low side, between 1200 and 1400 calories, you may need to increase them by 100–200 for 2–4 weeks to see if that improves things. Add the extra calories to your breakfast, or to your dinner if your dinner has been very small, and see if you start to regularly feel hungry again – hunger is a powerful sign that your metabolism may be picking up again.

If you have been enjoying a more liberal number of calories, say 1600–1800 calories, you may need to cut back for 2–4 weeks to see whether you actually need fewer calories now that you have lost weight. It is best to cut these calories from your evening meal or your snacks, leaving your breakfast and midday meal containing the bulk of your calories. The average 70 kilo woman needs 1400–1600 calories per day, but if you look at the calorie recommendations on food packages, you will see that they are much higher. This is one of the reasons why we often think we need a lot more than we actually do.

Change things around

If altering your calorie intake doesn't work, try changing the size of your meals and eat them at different times of the day. For example, you might switch to having 3 main meals rather than 6 small meals throughout the day, or you might halve the size of your dinner but increase the size of your lunch. It doesn't matter how you do it – change is the key. Generally speaking, though, the more calories you consume during the first half of the day, the better, which means having an early and reasonably large breakfast and lunch by 12 pm or 1 pm, and then lightening it up in the afternoon. Or it may mean making sure that you eat your dinner earlier; or, if you have already been having a very small dinner for some time, you may need to increase it a little.

As most people will only be consuming between 1200 and 1800 calories each day, you can see that, although we can change things around to give our metabolism a boost, there is a limit to what can be achieved by adjusting your food intake. By far the most effective way of boosting our metabolic rate and burning more calories is to change around the type, quantity and intensity of our training. All too often weight loss clients are going to the gym regularly or walking each day but are not training intensely enough to be burning a significant number of calories, and hence are maintaining their weight rather than losing it. The good news is that this is also very easy to change.

Are you training or maintaining?

If you have trained for many years and are coming out of the gym or training session feeling as if you could do it all over again, you are not training hard enough. While working out and burning a few hundred calories over the course of an hour is great for overall fitness, health and wellbeing, to really increase your metabolic rate and get your body burning more efficiently you have to train it – hard. This means constantly pushing yourself, so that after a 20–30 minute session you are fatigued and have burnt the 200–300 calories you previously burnt over the course of an hour. Sure, for those people who have not trained before, it is important to go slowly and build up, but for those who already train regularly, if your weight loss has hit a plateau you may not be going hard enough.

Less is sometimes more

When you have been training as part of a weight loss program and getting good results, you may think that more is better, and so instead of going to the gym 3 times a week you start to go 5 times a week, and also add in a daily walk. If you find that despite this extra training you are still not losing weight, it is natural to feel frustrated and perhaps want to throw in the towel. As weight loss is a constant juggle between calories in and calories out, if you are limiting calories and then burning more calories by doing more activity, the difference between calories in and calories out may become too great and the metabolism may slow to conserve energy.

For this reason, doing less but more intensive training is sometimes a good way to burn a significant number of extra calories each day without triggering excessive hunger or creating too big a difference between calories consumed via food and calories expended during training. This is important in order to ensure that your body does not perceive the calorie restriction as a state of starvation and reduce your metabolic rate to conserve energy.

Simple changes to your workouts can make them significantly more effective. For example, a change in speed, incline or style of training is often all you need to burn hundreds of extra calories. Here are some suggestions.

WALKING

While walking can be an extremely effective calorie burner, it can also quickly become more of a stroll than a workout. Mix up your walking by taking a different route each time. Seek out as many hills and stairs as possible, and if you can manage it, alternate walking and running to give you a much higher heart rate and a much better burn as a result.

TREADMILL

Once you are able to walk at a certain speed, there are two things you can do: start to run or increase the incline. Few people utilise the incline option on the treadmill while also increasing the speed. Even if you have to hold on to do this, you will be burning far more calories than you would by walking on the flat.

BIKE

It is easy for the leg muscles to get used to the demands of the stationary bike or a spin-style class, so you need to monitor your heart rate closely. Change the speed and resistance on your bike regularly so that it places different demands on your body each and every time you ride.

ROWER

Often forgotten, the rower is a great piece of cardio equipment. It is a whole body exercise, which means it requires you to use more muscles, and so you burn more calories. Adding just 10 minutes on the rower to any of your cardio programs or classes will see you burn at least another 100 calories.

You are overtraining

Sometimes after a prolonged weight loss program during which you have been training intensely and eating well almost 100 per cent of the time, you simply need a break. This is likely to be the case if you have been training every single day for a number of hours as well as monitoring your calories very carefully for many months. Try cutting back to just 2–3 sessions a week and increase your calories slightly to see if that does the trick and gets you off your plateau. If not, you may need a complete break with just light walking to actually drop some muscle mass as well as fat, which will in turn see some weight loss on the scales.

Tips and tricks to help shift a plateau

- A weight loss plateau refers to a significant period of time (at least 3 weeks) in which you seem to be 'stuck' at a certain weight and unable to lose any more on your current calorie and exercise plan.

- The first thing to keep in mind is that weight loss plateaus are a normal part of the weight loss process and as such should be expected.

- In general, you are likely to experience a plateau if you have been following a weight loss program for a significant period of time (8–12 weeks) and/or have already lost a significant amount of weight (5–10 kilos).

- The reason why weight loss plateaus occur is that the body likes weight to be stable. After you have lost a significant amount of weight, the body becomes accustomed to a new, lower weight and wants to stabilise this weight and maintain it.

- The best thing you can do to shift yourself from a weight loss plateau is to change your routine by altering your calories and/ or the type and intensity of the training you are doing.

- Specifically, you can try increasing your calories by 100–200 a day, especially if you have been restricting yourself to 1200 calories a day for some time. If you have been enjoying more calories (1800 or more) a day, you can try cutting your daily intake by 100–200 calories a day for a week or two.

- With exercise, change is the key. For example, if you have been walking every day, you could try switching to a more intense form of training such as hill or stair climbing rather than walking on the flat. You could also change the time of day that you train; for example, training after dinner rather than before breakfast.

- When the word 'plateau' is heard so often in weight loss circles, you may think you are experiencing a plateau when in fact you may simply need to be a little stricter with your diet and training. To make sure you are experiencing a plateau, remember to log your calories online regularly and to monitor the intensity of your training sessions.

- Finally, once you have made the necessary changes, you will need to wait at least another week before you start to see any change on the scales, so try and be patient.

Bouncing back after a weight loss relapse

Arrrgghhhhh!! Why is it so hard to lose weight but so easy to put it on again? Unfortunately, this is a reality that none of us is ever likely to change, because after millions of years of evolution the human body is programmed to store fat in case of famine, a state admittedly not as likely now as it was thousands of years ago. If you also consider that it is much easier to overeat than undereat and that in our society food is around us all the time, it is pretty clear why it is so easy to gain weight in general, let alone after you have lost it.

A weight loss relapse, when you regain a significant amount of the weight you had lost, is extremely common. There are many factors that can be linked to a relapse. By far the most common is that many people who commit to losing weight see it as a short-term commitment. They make the effort to lose weight, and then once it is gone they quickly revert to their old diet and exercise habits – the very habits that saw them gain weight in the first place. Almost as common a factor is that, because we have such ready access to food, we are all likely to be gaining weight, especially but not only as we get older, unless we keep on top of our diet and exercise regimes most of the time. Such self-regulation requires a degree of self-monitoring and discipline that many of us struggle with in modern life. And then there are the scenarios in which an intense life event, whether it be getting married or divorced, having a baby, losing a job or dealing with a trauma, forces you to focus on other issues for a period of time and your diet and exercise regime falls by the wayside.

The reason why weight loss becomes more difficult after each relapse is that as we get older our cells work less efficiently, which means that our metabolism slows down. When cells are exposed to this 'weight loss, weight regain' cycle time and time again, their efficiency is repeatedly challenged, and this explains why a strict regime that may have worked for you once or even twice no longer produces the same results. Because the body is now less efficient at processing fuel, you now have to put in even more effort than you did previously to implement the specific food intake patterns and exercise regimes that will kick-start things and get the cells burning fuel optimally again. So the less weight you regain and the sooner you get back on track after things have gone haywire, the better.

While it is by far the best idea to keep yourself on track and avoid relapses, in reality they do occur from time and time and so you need to know what to do if you find yourself in this situation. The first thing you need to do is to ask yourself why it happened.

Was it . . .
Laziness?
A lack of self-monitoring?
A change of routine?
A change of season?
Poor planning?
Too many celebrations?
Not enough training?
Events outside your control?
A medical issue?
An injury?

The truth is that the majority of these factors are things that you will have had some degree of control over. In those cases you need to accept responsibility for what happened, and also to accept that eating largely calorie-controlled foods and exercising regularly are things you are going to have to do on most days for the rest of your life if you are to avoid gaining weight. If you have battled weight in the past, you also need to accept that unless you commit to monitoring your weight, training and calorie intake on a regular basis, weight will gradually creep back on whether you like it or not.

Once you have identified the primary reason why you regained weight, it is time to get serious. You will need to go in hard to give your body the kick-start it requires to shift into fat-burning mode. Unfortunately, this means that you may have to be stricter than you were before. You may need to try a protein shake regime for a week or two, or invest in a personal trainer for a 3 month period to ensure you train really hard and give your body the metabolic shake-up it may need. Next, you need to devise a weight loss regime that is sustainable for you personally, so that you don't set yourself up to repeat this process in the future. This may mean, for example, changing your dietary approach or finding a cheaper form of training so that you can afford it in the long term. Finally but perhaps most importantly, if you have lost weight and regained it numerous times throughout your life, it may be time to seek some professional psychological advice to help you understand why you keep relapsing and to determine if there are any underlying psychological issues preventing you from gaining control over your weight in the long term.

Cultivating a weight loss mindset

❧ *I do not want to hear why you can't; I am only interested in why you can.*

If you have lost weight, especially a lot of weight, and then put all or most of it back on again, chances are you are feeling pretty bad about it. You wouldn't be human if you didn't. While feeling bad can help to motivate you to move forward, emotions such as guilt, frustration and disappointment are unlikely to be helpful and need to be kept in check. You know you have dropped the ball and undone some or all of your hard work, but the good news is that you can change things. The key is not to dwell on 'woulda, shoulda, coulda' thoughts but to focus solely on moving forward. Once you have reflected on where you went wrong last time, you are done with the past and it is time to let go.

It is challenging to move forward when you are feeling negative about yourself, as the negative thoughts can virtually block out the positive thoughts that will help you develop a plan to achieve what you want to achieve. If you are someone who constantly battles negative thoughts, particularly in relation to losing weight and keeping it off in the long term, you simply must learn to manage these thoughts. We all have positive and negative thoughts, but positive people are better able to manage the negative ones and don't get overwhelmed by them.

In order to gain control over negative thoughts, you have to practise, practise, practise. Each and every time you have a thought that is questioning your ability to lose weight and keep it off, practise responding with the same mantra: 'I will lose weight; there is nothing that can stop me from losing weight this time'. You may need to repeat this mantra a hundred times, you may need to repeat it a thousand times, but until it becomes deeply entrenched in your psyche you will remain vulnerable and will be at risk of returning to your old habits.

BLOCK OUT A MONTH

A month out of a lifetime is not a long time, yet it is enough to see some real results and give your metabolism a good kick-start after a period of abuse. A month is enough to see you lose 3–5 kilos, to shift your mood and mindset back to that of someone who is losing weight, and to regain control of your life. The reason that people who attend weight loss retreats or 'boot camps' manage to achieve so much is that they are able to focus solely and completely on weight loss for that period of time.

Ideally, choose a time when you have few social commitments and work is manageable. Schedule in your training sessions and time to prepare the foods you need to stay on track. Allow yourself more sleep than you usually would, and book in self-care activities such as massages for times when you would usually socialise. Use the down time to reflect on the many benefits of finally getting your weight under control and to plan for the future. Gaining control of your weight can be one of the most transformational changes you will ever go through in life, so pay attention to your mood and feelings throughout this time and try to enjoy the process and the clarity it brings.

GO IN HARD WITH THE CALORIES

Yoyo dieters have no choice but to be strict with their calories. No more extras, no more 'I just had a taste', no more rubbish. It is time to fuel your body with nutritious, good-quality food and to let go of your bad food habits once and for all.

It often surprises people to be told that overweight people generally don't eat all that much high-fat food; rather they simply eat a lot more, all the time. A snack here, a nibble there, and before you know it there are too many calories being ingested and weight is increasing.

Controlling your calorie intake on a daily basis requires self-regulation – the ability to say no, and to stop when you need to. To know when you have had enough and when it is time to put the knife and fork down. Seasoned dieters are notoriously bad at doing this, and will need to go back to the basics of calorie counting to be reminded once again of where they so often go wrong when trying to lose weight.

If you know you have been consuming too many calories, start your new regime with a moderate calorie intake of 1400–1500 calories. If, however, you feel as though you need a real kick-start, try 1200–1300 calories for a week or two. Remember that changing your calorie intake around throughout your program is one of the keys to losing weight, and try not to follow a 1200 calorie plan for any longer than 4–6 weeks.

INVEST IN A TRAINER
If there was a perfect time to invest in a trainer, a diet and/or exercise relapse would be it. Not only is it crucial to be motivated at this time, but to really kick-start weight loss you also need to train hard, really hard, for a period of time. A trainer keeps you accountable, knows how to push you in the right way and is a great way to cement initial changes when you embark on a new program.

IDENTIFY YOUR TRIGGERS

We all have certain triggers that send us off track, whether it is a negative interaction with another person, stress, tempting food environments or food-focused social lives, but ultimately you do need to learn to manage yourself in these environments if you are to gain control over your weight in the long term. You also need to develop contingency plans for all situations likely to trigger a relapse, so that you know exactly what to do to avoid going off the rails.

TRIGGER	RESPONSE YOU NEED TO PRACTISE
Stress	Don't reach for food to comfort yourself; do something else (such as listen to music, go for a walk, ring a friend).
Boredom	Keep busy; find a new hobby or pastime.
Loneliness	Get out and socialise.
Unhappiness	Identify things that make you happy and do more of them.
Distraction	Practise being mindful of your food and activity needs.

SET UP SYSTEMS

People who control their weight have a few things in common, and one of them is creating an environment around them that helps them to keep on track. This may mean asking your mother-in-law to look after the children so that you can go to the gym, or negotiating flexible working hours so that you can fit in your training. It may be cooking the week's meals in advance or shopping online so that the fresh food you need to eat well is always on hand. Each person will go about things in their own way, but the important thing is to develop strategies that allow you to negotiate the daily struggle with work, family and traffic as well as to eat well and fit in your regular training sessions.

To help you identify the strategies that will work for you, consider the key people in your life who may be able to help you at different times. Who do you need more support from, and have you asked for it? Sometimes we are reluctant to ask those closest to us for help, as we feel they ought to know that we need help and offer it. It is time to recognise that idealistic scenario for what it is and to ask for help when you need it. If you need your partner to get up earlier and help with the kids in the morning so that you can go for a run, ask them. If you need your mother or father to cook a meal for the family once a week so that you can go to the gym, ask them. What is the worst that can happen? Ultimately, mobilising your key support team, whether it is your partner, another family member or your best friend, or all three, is one of the key strategies that will enable you to prioritise your health and food and exercise needs on a daily basis.

ALLOW 3 MONTHS

Once you have gained some momentum and feel as though you are back on track with your weight loss, it is essential to stay focused for at least 3 months. On average it takes 3 months to cement any new habit, and so you will need this time to establish the eating and exercise habits that are to form the basis of your new lifestyle. In 3 months you can lose at least 5–10 kilos, which will help you to feel that you are back in control of your body and your life.

While it is impossible to avoid all social contact during this time, it is wise to try and limit your indulgences, whether food or alcohol, to just one occasion each week and to keep holidays and other significant social commitments to a minimum. While this may seem a bit extreme, if you reflect on the stress your weight regain has caused you and the commitment required to make major lifestyle changes yet again, you will soon see that it makes eminently good sense. By now it should also have started to resonate with you that going off the rails when it comes to diet and exercise is simply not worth it. **Ask yourself: Do I really want to put my mind and my body through all this again?**

When it may be insulin resistance

❧ *No matter what I do, I cannot seem to lose weight.'*

While it is the goal of many people to lose weight, and preferably lose it fast, there is one increasingly common clinical condition that can make weight loss extremely difficult. Although no official statistics are available, evidence suggests that up to 20–30 per cent of adults have a degree of insulin resistance, a condition that significantly impedes the body's natural ability to burn body fat in accordance with the energy balance equation.

For many years, scientists, nutritionists and numerous other weight loss professionals have continually preached that weight loss comes down to a very simple equation – calories in versus calories out. While this principle is true to a certain extent, a number of increasingly common hormonal shifts that alter this relationship can occur. Insulin resistance, the clinical condition that precedes Type 2 diabetes, is one such diagnosis. People with insulin resistance can struggle to lose weight via traditional weight loss methods simply because their body is not burning fat the way it should be.

Insulin is a hormone secreted by the pancreas and used to digest carbohydrates. Carbohydrates are found in plant-based foods, including bread, rice, breakfast cereals, pasta, fruits and sugars. When carbohydrate-rich foods are consumed, the pancreas secretes insulin, which transports glucose from the food to the muscles to be burnt as energy. Over time, however, insulin may fail to work as well as it should.

When things go wrong

There are a number of reasons why things may go wrong. Weight gain, which results in fat clogging the cells and preventing insulin from taking glucose into the cells, is one reason, and a lack of physical activity, which results in the muscles becoming less efficient at burning glucose, is another. While your genetic make-up can predispose you to insulin resistance, the highly processed nature of the carbohydrates many of us consume daily, including breads, breakfast cereals and snack foods, which require much higher amounts of insulin than less processed, low glycemic index (GI) carbohydrates, is also thought to be a significant contributing factor in the increased incidence of insulin resistance.

Insulin resistance develops over time when high glucose levels from a diet high in processed carbohydrates as well as inactivity result in increased secretion of insulin. Over time, for the various reasons mentioned above, the cells build up a resistance to insulin, which results in the body gradually producing more and more insulin in an attempt to get it to continue to transport glucose to the body's cells for energy. This cycle in which insulin is working overtime may continue unnoticed for many years, since there are few symptoms associated with high insulin levels, as the body aggressively compensates to ensure that glucose levels are kept tightly regulated.

From a weight loss perspective, what is important to know is that another key function of insulin in the body is to prevent fat being burnt in order to preserve both muscle and fat mass. This means that the greater the amount of insulin that is circulating in the body, the harder it will be to burn body fat. So a person with insulin resistance will find it harder to lose weight, as the high insulin levels are working against them even though they may be restricting their calorie intake, controlling their carbohydrate intake and getting sufficient exercise. High levels of insulin can also make you feel tired and bloated and give you sugar cravings, as the cells are not processing the glucose they need to provide energy.

Signs that you may have a degree of insulin resistance include an inability to lose weight despite demonstrated diet and exercise compliance, distinct abdominal fat, feeling unusually fatigued, bloated and experiencing sugar cravings. To check for insulin resistance you need to see your GP or endocrinologist and have a glucose tolerance test, as the condition may require medication and further medical management.

Managing insulin resistance

The good news is that once diagnosed by a physician or endocrinologist, insulin resistance can be managed, and careful management can prevent the development of Type 2 diabetes. While some cases will warrant medication, the diet and exercise prescription is the same for everyone. People who are insulin resistant need a reduced carbohydrate, increased protein diet as developed by a dietitian who specialises in the area, as well as a highly specific training program that integrates high-intensity cardio sessions with a resistance training program. They also need to learn to become extremely fussy about their choice of carbohydrate foods. High GI, refined sources of carbohydrates, including juices, white breads and refined cereals, need to be eliminated from the diet in the long term, and this will also produce the best weight loss outcome in the long term.

In terms of the diet and exercise information in *Lose Weight Fast*, the general diet plans for each program contain 30–40 per cent protein, which means that they are suitable for people with insulin resistance (IR), although the results will be a lot slower. For example, if a person without IR can lose 1–2 kilos a week, a person with IR will be lucky to lose this in a month. However, while the initial 5–10 kilos will be lost slowly, over a 3–6 month period insulin sensitivity will improve and weight loss may speed up. It is still strongly suggested that you work closely with your own endocrinologist and dietitian to get the best results for your own individual needs.

Regaining your life post weight loss

❖ *At some point you will stop having a weight issue, and that is nothing but liberating, both physically and psychologically.*

Weight loss is not just about losing weight, it is about regaining control of your body, your health and ultimately your life. For those who have had weight issues for some time, or who felt that their weight was holding them back in life in some way, losing a significant amount of weight can be the start of some major life changes.

The first thing to keep in mind, especially if you have lost more than 10 kilos, is that you need to take things slowly. Unfortunately, weight regain is extremely common, so you need to concentrate on maintaining your new food and exercise habits long term, not just for a few extra weeks or months once you perceive that you have 'finished' the program.

All too often excess weight is a marker for other things that are going on in our lives. Now you have successfully lost weight it is an opportune time to consider some of your other life domains and ensure they too are on track to support your new lean life.

Are you happy?

Happiness is a broad description that we give to a range of emotions and feelings and can differ widely on a day-to-day basis, but overall we are referring to a general feeling of fulfilment and happiness in terms of our general life direction. That is, whether we are happy with our relationships, job, friends, interests, work–life balance – the individual components that make up our lives.

An easy way to gauge your underlying happiness and sense of fulfilment is to consider how you feel when you are going to bed at night as well as when you first wake up in the morning. If you end many days each week with a feeling of relief and exhaustion, or start the day with a feeling of trepidation and dread, chances are that there are some areas of your life that need some work. Of course there are stages in everyone's life when change is needed but if such feelings are widespread across a number of your life areas, it may be a sign that some major decisions are pending, decisions that will ultimately propel you towards a state of greater happiness and fulfilment.

Such big questions may seem overwhelming, but remember that there is no rush. These feelings of unfulfilment and unhappiness are simply nudging you to consider some changes, changes that you can make in your own time, but the first step towards change is acknowledging these feelings and taking some time to explore them.

Every day we need to wake up and know what we are doing that will help move us towards our bigger picture goals, before the days slip away.

Core life domains

When working with clients, one technique that can be useful is to break down life change into the various core life domains – relationships, financial, career and self-care. Now, as you have spent a significant number of the past few months working on health and fitness, you may have identified that other areas of your life are also in need of some work. To brainstorm some changes that may be needed to help move your life forward, simply invest in a journal and start to make some notes about things you know you need to do within each of these domains. For example, you may need to see a financial planner, or complete some extra study to further your career. You may need to widen your social circle to make some new friends, or commit to a new hobby. There are no rules, but starting to consider each area of your life and the way you could add or improve each one is a great structural way to take control, give yourself some clear direction and improve your happiness and wellbeing in the long term.

RELATIONSHIPS

Our relationships include both our intimate and non-intimate relationships. You may be looking for a new partner or looking to widen your friendship circle. You may need to give more quality time to your relationships or strike more of a balance between your work and your personal life.

Our relationships can bring the greatest joy to our lives but also the most pain. Like all things in life, relationships change, and sometimes when we have not prepared for the change we can cling to relationships that we should move on from. The most common issue with relationships is that they become unbalanced – one partner is giving more to the relationship than the other, and as such resentment builds and the relationship is unable to continue to flow in an even, reciprocal fashion.

If you feel as though you are constantly giving to some of your relationships, whether in your intimate or non-intimate interactions, and it is not being reciprocated, it may be time to consider if you are giving too much, or more importantly how you can focus on attracting people into your life who are able to give you what you need in a friendship, partnership or relationship. If you consider that we ultimately teach others how we should be treated, it really is up to us to seek out those who support us and nurture our souls as opposed to those who we spend time with out of habit or obligation.

People who should be in our lives bring us joy and happiness, while those who bring us stress, grief and anxiety should not, and if there are a few of those hanging around in your world, it may be time to seek out some new friends and/or a new partner to ensure long-term happiness.

If you know that you need some new people in your world, the best action you can take is to get out there. Join a new club, accept invitations when you would usually be inclined to stay at home, and set up some online dates. Sometimes meeting a few new people is all you need to be reminded that there are many other interesting people out there for you to spend time with, and who enjoy your company. There are no rules that say you have to marry the person you meet on a date, or that you have to see new people you meet ever again, but meeting new people after you have been in a rut is simply a way to bring new energy into your world, and new energy is often all we need to help us move forward.

FINANCIAL

Managing your finances, having financial goals and ultimately becoming financially secure offers great overall security as well as giving you far greater control over what you do and when you do it.

To work towards financial security, you may need to take greater interest in your finances, you may need to earn more money, or you may simply need to learn to manage your money better, but being in control of your finances can be almost as empowering as taking control of your weight.

Simple daily steps such as making a budget and sticking to it, keeping track of your spending or making a plan to pay off a credit card can instantly lower your stress levels and free you from the constant financial worry that plagues so many people for so much of their lives. And the good thing about financial planning is that it tends to involve far fewer emotions than relationships and weight control, and therefore can be an easy place to start making changes.

CAREER

So many of us spend so much of our lives working for 50 or 60 hours each week at a job we hate – it is no wonder so many of us eat, gain weight and feel depressed. Now, career change is no minor thing, and of course there are many things to consider when you are looking at a change of jobs or even career, including financial and family commitments, income levels and job availability, but if you do dread going to work practically every single day, your heart and your mind are trying to tell you something.

In the interim, or until you are ready physically and psychologically to change jobs or careers, on a day-to-day basis at least try to make the working week as enjoyable as possible. Get out of the office at lunchtime to run errands or do something nice to nurture your soul, be as productive as possible, and try not to take on board any stress or negative emotions from those around you – it is not likely to be worth it.

If job change is not a real possibility for you, this means that your personal life and free time must be filled with much pleasure and enjoyment.

SELF-CARE

A lack of time and care for oneself is common in those who battle weight issues. It takes energy and time to give your body and your mind the physical and emotional support it needs to be at its best in a stressful world. Men are much better at self-care than women, and mothers are the worst of all. Our weight, mood and body suffer when we do not practise it, and it can be a hard habit to build and maintain.

The mistake that many of us make when it comes to self-care is that we do not prioritise our own needs, instead giving everything to others before we consider caring for ourselves. The downside of this approach is that we are left tired, exhausted, fat and resentful while we are also teaching others that this scenario is okay, so that children, husbands, friends and family continue to expect the level of care we give them.

A much better approach is to ensure that at the very least you are practising some basic self-care on a daily, weekly and monthly basis so as to not only give yourself the energy you need to be at your best, but also to care for your body and your health.

If you know that you need to work on your own self-care, here are some ideas to start with:

- Try to arrange at least one fun social event each week.

- Aim to do one nice thing for yourself each week.

- Aim for at least some alone time with your partner each month.

- Schedule at least one exercise session each week.

- Plan at least one break or holiday to look forward to each year.

Once you create these breaks in your day, your week and your life, you will be surprised how much better you feel, and how much more time and energy you have to make the effort to eat well.

Small things

When we emerge from a period of change, motivation tends to be high and things appear to be going well. As time moves on, day-to-day life gradually starts to take over, and before we know it we can be back in the cycle of 'just getting through the day' and back into our old habits, often habits that are not conducive to weight control.

In an attempt to prevent such a scenario reoccurring, being mindful of deriving pleasure on a day-to-day basis from the small things is a crucial part of happiness and wellbeing.

Taking time to look at the flowers when you walk each day, or having a cheerful conversation with the man who makes your coffee in the morning, creating a 'sacred space' at home where you read your book each night before you go to bed, or having a fun lunch date once each week with one of your favourite people – often it is the small, seemingly insignificant interactions with others on a daily basis that create the joy of life, and sometimes we do need to be reminded of this to make an effort to savour these moments more fully.

Acceptance

The sooner we work towards acceptance in our lives the sooner we start to pave our way to happiness and wellbeing: accepting that at times things will be good, and at times things will be not so good; accepting that we have to work hard to eat well and look after our body; accepting whatever the world presents us with and then dealing with it in the best way we know how. Acceptance brings inner peace, and that is ultimately what we all hope for. Once you have that, you have everything.

Acknowledgements

To my wonderful agent Pippa Masson, and publisher Mark Lewis, for not only believing in what we can do together, but for being so fabulous to work with in general – I could not ask for better people.

To the entire team at Random House, from marketing to publicity and everything in between. Thank you for making this book all it could be and for ensuring the process ran as smoothly as possible.

To my loyal group of friends who bring me so much joy and unconditional support on a daily basis: Possy, Helen, Naoms, JFL, Trader, Sharron, Kylie, Mary, Janine and Todd. Every day I am grateful that you are in my life.

To my family – Jeff, Mum and my IT/emotional/business/family dinner night support team Stef and Jacq, this is as much your work as it is mine.

And finally to the love of my life, my darling B, for getting me through Thursdays and every day in between – thank God you're here.